Reflections Of A Wary Samaritan

Reflections Of A Wary Samaritan

Farrell F Neeley PhD

Copyright © 2016 Farrell F Neeley PhD
All rights reserved.

ISBN: 099062563X
ISBN 13: 9780990625636

Table of Contents

Author's Preface ································xxv

Chapter 1································1

   Jesus Talks About The Good Samaritan ················1

   The Toll Taken ·····································3

   Education Of A Wary Samaritan ······················6

   Keep Your Tools Sharp ·····························7

   No Good Deed Goes Unpunished ····················8

   The Rest Is Up To You ·····························8

   Give A Man A Fish ································10

   I've Seen The Sausage Made ························13

   Here Am I, Send Me ······························14

    Value Of Authenticity · 15

    Forget The Lone Ranger Approach · · · · · · · · · · · · · · · · · · 16

    What's In It for Me · 17

Chapter 2 · **19**

    A Wary Samaritan's Prayer · 19

    Learning And Moving On · 19

    You Don't Have To Be A Boy Scout · · · · · · · · · · · · · · · · · · 21

    Recharging Your Soul · 22

    Where Nobody Knows Your Name · · · · · · · · · · · · · · · · · · · 22

    Reading The Obituaries · 24

    Caveat Emptor – Good Samaritan Beware · · · · · · · · · · · · · 25

    What's Your Hidden Talent · 27

    The "It Takes A Village" Good Samaritan · · · · · · · · · · · · · 28

    Encouraging The Wary Samaritans · · · · · · · · · · · · · · · · · · · 30

    Rescuing Ourselves · 31

    Unsung Heroes And Heroines · 32

    Do As I Do, Not As I Say · 34

    Rolling With The Punches · 34

Chapter 3 ·36

Gary Brown ·36

Look Before You Leap ·37

Starve A Dozen ·38

What Will the Neighbors Think · · · · · · · · · · · · · · · · ·39

Sometimes The Victim Won't Cooperate · · · · · · · · · · · · · ·39

Neighborhood Good Samaritan · · · · · · · · · · · · · · · · · · ·40

Teach Your Children Well ·40

Wary But Willing ·41

We Won't Be Fooled Again ·41

Can They Be Trusted ·42

Be Wary, Not Heartless ·43

Critics Of The Good Samaritan · · · · · · · · · · · · · · · · · · ·45

Spotting Hidden Need ·47

Moving Toward The Danger ·49

Sometimes Five Minutes Is Enough · · · · · · · · · · · · · · · ·50

Small Acts Of Kindness ·51

Start At Home ·51

Chapter 4 ·52

   The Locusts Or The Satellite ·52

   Are You Planting A Garden ·54

   Avoiding The Spotlight ·54

   Pencils Or Bullets ·56

   I Can't Go There Anymore ·57

   Who Gains And Who Loses? ·59

   Good Deed Multiplication ·60

   Are You Wary Enough ·60

   I Can't Treat Dead ·62

   In Hindsight ·63

   If You Give Your Body To Be Burned · · · · · · · · · · · · · · · · · ·64

   It's A Good Thing ·64

   Kick It Up A Notch ·64

   Finding An Alternative Good Work · · · · · · · · · · · · · · · · · · ·65

   Beggars Versus The Needy ·66

   Good Samaritans Outnumber Thieves · · · · · · · · · · · · · · · · ·67

   He Wasn't The Perfect Samaritan ·68

Chapter 5 70

    Give Gifts With Lasting Meaning 70

    Learning And Teaching New Tricks 71

    It's Still The Small Details 72

    Be Wary Of The Pretenders 73

    I've Been Taken Again 74

    Placing Your Life At Risk 75

    Well Done 76

    People Just Needing A Break 77

    Would You Do It For Jesus 77

    Sufficient To The Day Is The Evil Thereof 78

    Knowledge Area Experts 79

    Practical Good Samaritanism 80

    Don't Get Fooled Again 81

    A Tiny Vision 81

    Hidden Benefactors 82

    How We Come To Be Wary Samaritans 83

    Too Much Analyses And Speculation 85

Action Speaks Louder Than Words · · · · · · · · · · · · · · · · · · ·85

Stand By Me ·85

Chapter 6 ·87

Mildred Collins ·87

Miracles Are Within Your Power ·91

Improving Your Wary Samaritan Perception · · · · · · · · · · · ·91

Volunteer's Remorse ·93

Too Wary A Good Samaritan ·93

Unexpected Good Samaritan ·94

Go Easy On Yourself ·95

Unwelcome Warnings ·95

Make Space For Others ·96

Sometimes You Better Drive On Past · · · · · · · · · · · · · · · · · ·97

Sharing Our Knowledge Is Sharing Ourselves · · · · · · · · · · ·97

A Minute To Catch Your Breath ·98

A Wary Samaritan Knows No Holidays · · · · · · · · · · · · · · · ·98

Children Need Good Samaritans Too · · · · · · · · · · · · · · · · ·99

The Need At Hand · 100

Wary Samaritan Sense · 100

Must I Fight You To Help You · 101

Searching For The Fire · 102

Babysitting Good Samaritans · 102

From One Fire To The Next · 103

Crashing And Repairing Your Hard Drive · · · · · · · · · · · · · 104

What Compels You · 105

Be Aware, Stay Aware · 105

Kindness Today · 106

Practitioners Of Personal Evil · 106

Works Of Faith · 107

Heart Of A Good Samaritan · 107

Justice Cometh And That Right Soon · · · · · · · · · · · · · · · 108

Unhappy Needy People · 109

Giving Just A Little · 111

Never Judge Another Wary Samaritan · · · · · · · · · · · · · · · 111

An Inconvenient Time · 112

Con Artists Of Every Stripe · 112

Bad Samaritans · 114

Keep Your Heart Open To Children · · · · · · · · · · · · · · · · · 115

Give It Away · 116

Chapter 7 · **118**

Are You Qualified · 118

Lizard Traps · 119

Volunteer Opportunities · 121

A Wary Samaritan At Home · 122

Meeting Your Master's Expectations · · · · · · · · · · · · · · · · · 123

Good Samaritans And Good Neighbors · · · · · · · · · · · · · · 124

Accepting The Good Samaritan · 125

Casting Bread Upon The Water · 125

More Than Enough Need To Go Around · · · · · · · · · · · · 126

Prepared To Be A Good Samaritan · · · · · · · · · · · · · · · · · · 126

Train Up A Child · 128

You Can't Take It With You ·129

Going With Grace ·130

Maybe They're The Crazy Ones ·131

This Isn't Dial-A-Prayer ·132

Inconvenient ·132

Donor Beware ·133

I Could Learn To Live With It ·133

Working The Lot ·134

Not A Heartless Samaritan ·134

Chapter 8 ·**137**

Ten Things The Good Samaritan Never Said · · · · · · · · · ·137

Fools Rush In ·138

Another Clever Idea For Good Samaritans · · · · · · · · · · · ·138

Cautious Strangers ·139

Weary In Well-Doing ·140

Become Engaged ·140

We All Need A Good Samaritan Sometime · · · · · · · · · · · ·141

The Times They Are A Changin' ·142

Lacking Compassion ·143

Weighing My Day ·145

Self-Absorbed ·145

Doing Well By Doing Good ·145

It's A Big Deal To The Recipient ·146

Good Deeds Are Not Always Obvious · · · · · · · · · · · · · · · · ·146

Policeman Good Samaritan ·146

Broadcasting False Signals Of Benevolence · · · · · · · · · · · ·147

Shared Missions ·148

Cautious Good Samaritan ·148

A Messed Up And Deadly World ·149

Road Hazard ·150

Christmas Is Coming And Con Artists Will
Soon Upon Us ·151

Maybe You Should Consider A Divorce · · · · · · · · · · · · · · ·151

Who Dropped The Ball ·153

Chapter 9 · 154

    Anna "Neeley" Rogers · 154

    Good Deeds Are More Important Now Than Ever · · · · · · 156

    Power In Smiles And Kind Words · · · · · · · · · · · · · · · · · · 157

    We All Need Beautiful Music · 157

    A Good Samaritan's Integrity · 158

    Take A Break · 159

    Help Is On The Way · 160

    Brighten Someone's Day · 161

    In Some Way Inconvenient · 162

    Secret Good Samaritan · 162

    Words Of Encouragement · 163

    Check Before You Hit "Send" · 163

    Sharing You · 164

    No Small Kindnesses · 165

    Sharing Traffic Lanes · 165

    Lowered Expectations · 166

Killing Me Isn't Part Of The Good
Samaritan Paradigm ·167

Living In Garbage ·168

Sharing The Knowledge You Possess · · · · · · · · · · · · · · · ·169

Make Someone's Day· ·170

Good Deeds Aren't Hypothetical · · · · · · · · · · · · · · · · · ·170

Almost Overwhelming· ·171

No Good Samaritan's Remorse Today · · · · · · · · · · · · · ·171

Chapter 10 ·**172**

Huong Thi Tran: "I Never Forget This Lesson" · · · · · · · ·172

More Than Poppies· ·174

At Home First· ·175

Wary Doesn't Mean Despairing · · · · · · · · · · · · · · · · · · ·175

Modern Day Acts of Kindness· · · · · · · · · · · · · · · · · · · ·176

It Was No Big Deal· ·176

Stealthy Good Samaritanism· ·177

An Age Of False Prophets ·178

Facilitators Of Insight · 179

Check Out That Charity · 180

An Immigrant's Dream · 180

Pick Your Own Charities · 181

Know Your Trash, Know Your Treasures · · · · · · · · · · · · · · 182

Chapter 11 · 184

Alton 'Tony' Engel · 184

Some Gave All · 185

Keep Both Eyes Open · 186

Identify Your Villains And Move On · · · · · · · · · · · · · · · · · · 187

Take Care Of Yourself · 187

Some Days Many... Some Days Few · · · · · · · · · · · · · · · · · · 188

There Are No Small Good Deeds · 188

Charities And Survival Of The Fittest · · · · · · · · · · · · · · · · · 188

Thy Weaker Brother · 189

Finding Energy In The Good Works Of Others · · · · · · · · 190

Move Along With Your Cheap Drivel · · · · · · · · · · · · · · · · 190

Animals Need Good Samaritans Too · · · · · · · · · · · · · · · · · ·191

Sharing And Receiving Knowledge · · · · · · · · · · · · · · · · · ·192

Opportunities To Serve· ·192

It's Demanding To Be A Good Samaritan · · · · · · · · · · · · ·193

Stealthy Samaritans Take Care ·194

Never Counting The Cost ·194

He Led With His Heart· ·195

How Will Others Be Affected ·195

Wary Of Myself· ·196

Rough Patches, Potholes, And Bridges Washed Out· · · · ·197

Bitter Good Samaritans· ·198

Allow God To Be The Judge ·199

Suddenly A Victim ·199

Supporting Roles ·200

Chapter 12· ·202

Engage And Remain Engaged ·202

Trolls With You Always· ·203

Staying Ahead Of The Trolls · 204

Best Supporting Good Samaritan · · · · · · · · · · · · · · · · · · · 204

I'm Not Pollyanna · 205

Not Always An Easy Thing · 206

Facebook® Panhandlers · 206

Compelled To Good Samaritanism · · · · · · · · · · · · · · · · · 208

Critics And Rejection · 209

Take A Closer Look · 210

Accept And Celebrate You · 211

Good Samaritans In Every City · 212

Something Positive In The Air · 212

Unsung Heroes · 212

Children Of The Same Creator · 213

Doing Nothing At All · 214

Social Media Con Artists · 214

Please Check The Math · 216

Lighten Up On Yourself · 217

Chapter 13 218

    Otto Davis 218

    Sometimes Only Words 221

    For All The Good You Do 222

    Good Deeds And Good Samaritans 222

    There's More Than One Kind Of Good Samaritan 222

    Action Not Words 223

    Blessed Is He Who Is Not Offended In Me 224

    No Less Important 225

    Allowing Others To Serve 225

    You Could Lose Your Good Samaritans 226

    Blessed Are The Peacemakers 226

    The True Good Samaritans 227

    Lending Them A Helping Hand 227

    Watch For The Quiet Ones 228

    Avoid Her At All Costs 230

    Needs In Front Of Your Face 230

Life's Hard Questions ·231

Recognizing Other's Good Works · · · · · · · · · · · · · · · · · · ·231

Look Before You Leap ·232

Horrible Things Sometimes Happen · · · · · · · · · · · · · · · · · ·232

Wisdom And Resolve Are Both Required · · · · · · · · · · · ·233

No Big Issues Here ·234

It's Not About You ·234

Examine Your Own Heart ·235

It's Their Decision… Good Or Bad · · · · · · · · · · · · · · · · · ·236

The High Cost Of Friendship ·236

Diversity Of Good Deeds ·236

Gain A Friend ·237

Be Careful What You Say About The Dead · · · · · · · · · · · ·237

Chapter 14 ·239

The Most Wonderful And Dangerous Time
Of The Year · 239

Before The Holiday Madness Begins · · · · · · · · · · · · · · · · ·241

Welcoming Kinder Gentler Days ·242

A Time For Joy And Caution ·243

Holiday Bell Ringers ·243

Seasonal Good Samaritanism ·243

Receiving Goodwill ·244

No Room In The Inn ·244

Today It's Your Turn ·245

Good Works Improve Your Outlook · · · · · · · · · · · · · · · · · ·245

Don't Let This Day Pass ·246

The Hardest People To Reach Out To · · · · · · · · · · · · · · · ·246

All Year Long ·247

Christmas Is Definitely Over ·247

We Rarely Know ·247

New Year… New Opportunities ·248

Author's Afterward · **249**

Dedication

This is my third book and my hope of course is to publish many more. But in deciding who to dedicate this book to, I had to consider who among all my friends, all of whom I regard as Good Samaritans, were the person or persons who stood out for all the good they've done... and the beatings they've taken.

I've known Jess and Geovana Karr for over twenty years now. In that time I've lost count of the money, time, and personal effort they've quietly put out on other people in their efforts to make those other people's lives better. I've also lost count of the times I've seen other people use them and abuse their goodwill.

Jess says my own wary example has caused them to stop and think about their efforts. I've been pleased in the past few years to have seen them truly join the ranks of the wary Samaritans. I salute this change in their approach because I've never known two better people... and the world needs them desperately.

Author's Preface

I've been a Christian by personal choice now for more than 45 years. In those years I've had victories and defeats which were mirrored by personal highs and lows. There's been little which I see as remarkable about my journey, but I recall many others I've known along the way who were knocked down and chose to never rise back up again. Sometimes it was the lure of an old lifestyle, a call from an old addiction, or in the saddest cases of all it was men and women crushed when they'd tried to do good and were repeatedly struck to the ground for their efforts.

These actual or metaphorical groundings took many forms. They also came from all quarters. Christians tend to think in terms of "them and us" when their eyes cast about for enemies. I think it's normal and natural to expect to be attacked by your avowed enemies. What seems abnormal and unnatural is when you're attacked by people who are avowedly on your side. This is especially devastating to novice believers who are in the early years of adopting a Christian philosophy and working to build a life on the principles they're just learning. As a consequence of this devastation many not only abandon Good Samaritanism...

they abandon their Christian faith and the lifestyle which goes with it.

Every age has had a need for Good Samaritans. If you consider the Good Samaritan in Jesus' story in Luke's Gospel, he wasn't the first; he was just one of millions before and since. He enjoys the title by virtue of the story, but I suspect the lifestyle had been in existence for thousands of years before. In reflecting on all I knew I was forced to consider how so many had hung onto their values and their faith through the millennia while others collapsed under the burden. I also looked at my life and how I managed to survive a few tough spots and not collapse under the burden. The answers were somewhat surprising.

There'll be those who read this and immediately begin to think of the passage about "Putting on the whole armor of God." While I agree this concept is vitally important, I concluded there was more afoot to spiritual survival than just clinging to overarching concepts of truth, righteousness, the Gospel, faith, salvation, the Spirit, and the Word of God. Each of these larger truths has some very mundane factors associated with them which make them work; there is no magic in the mere words. The barest fundamentals of our faith become the foundation upon which we build our lives and our works.

It took me decades to learn a Good Samaritan could only exist, survive, and thrive under certain conditions. Namely that he or she had to regard him or herself as worthy of self-care, worthy of refusing to be abused by others in a misguided effort to do God's work, and worthy of personal survival; God wants us to live for him and not necessarily to die for him. It was a sobering and sad realization for me. As I began to consider the fallen comrades I'd known through the years, I could now see the sword by which they'd been dispatched. I vowed to one day offer insights… this book is the outgrowth of that vow.

Farrell F. Neeley, PhD
October 28, 2015

CHAPTER 1

Jesus Talks About The Good Samaritan

I want to thank the editing team for calling to my attention that I wrote this entire book without actually sharing the story of *The Good Samaritan*. For members of my generation it was such a seminal tale from childhood Sunday Schools that I often forget many people, especially our younger people, have never heard this story. Below you'll find the actual story taken from the 10th chapter of Luke's Gospel from the King James version of The Holy Bible.

The story should provide you with context as to where the whole idea of being a Good Samaritan comes from. It only provides us with the bare details of that encounter; it does so in about 300 words. I'm certain millions and millions of words have been written and spoken about this man by preachers and writers in the centuries since. The wary Samaritan ethos at the heart of this book has come to life over the passing years as millions have learned that being a Good Samaritan is not without its hardships or dangers.

> *"And, behold, a certain lawyer stood up, and tempted him, saying, Master, what shall I do to inherit eternal life?*

He said unto him, What is written in the law? how readest thou?

And he answering said, Thou shalt love the Lord thy God with all thy heart, and with all thy soul, and with all thy strength, and with all thy mind; and thy neighbor as thyself.

And he said unto him, Thou hast answered right: this do, and thou shalt live.

But he, willing to justify himself, said unto Jesus, And who is my neighbor?

And Jesus answering said, A certain man went down from Jerusalem to Jericho, and fell among thieves, which stripped him of his raiment, and wounded him, and departed, leaving him half dead.

And by chance there came down a certain priest that way: and when he saw him, he passed by on the other side.

And likewise a Levite, when he was at the place, came and looked on him, and passed by on the other side.

But a certain Samaritan, as he journeyed, came where he was: and when he saw him, he had compassion on him,

And went to him, and bound up his wounds, pouring in oil and wine, and set him on his own beast, and brought him to an inn, and took care of him.

And on the morrow when he departed, he took out two pence, and gave them to the host, and said unto him, Take care of him;

and whatsoever thou spendest more, when I come again, I will repay thee.

Which now of these three, thinkest thou, was neighbor unto him that fell among the thieves?

And he said, He that shewed mercy on him. Then said Jesus unto him, Go, and do thou likewise."

The Toll Taken

When I began to write this book in 2014 I ran a Google search on Good Samaritans killed or injured while trying to assist someone in need. I was stunned at the number of injuries and deaths I found in just the first few pages. In the two years since the first search, I regularly make the same search and invariably I find the same staggering examples of serious injuries and deaths suffered by Good Samaritans. Being a Good Samaritan is not for the faint of heart. Wary Samaritans are a special lot within the ranks of the Good Samaritans. They find the courage to enter the fray again and again, despite the knowledge the outcome may not be the one they expected. Some of them I'll write about here and some others I'll allude to. There are legions of them and most of their names will never be widely known except to God and those they've helped. I've come to understand the overarching truth of wary Samaritanism is the genuine elements of personal loss and personal risk which are involved.

This life is not about seeking cheap thrills or acting out dime-novel heroics. It's about ordinary people choosing to enter into extraordinary circumstances. It's about ordinary people stepping away from the usual course of their lives and into the course of another person or persons' life. It's about ordinary people going places they normally wouldn't go. It's about ordinary people meeting people they wouldn't normally meet. It's about ordinary people taking risks they normally wouldn't take. It's about ordinary people expending capital of multiple sorts in ways they normally wouldn't spend it. I've never bought into the notion Good Samaritans are super heroes. Having spoken to dozens over the years, I've yet to meet one who saw themselves as even a mere hero, much less a super hero.

In fact, if Good Samaritans were all comic book super heroes there really wouldn't be so much to consider in the actions they take. When a super hero dives into a raging stream to save a drowning child it wouldn't actually require much of a super hero's powers; it could require the life of the Good Samaritan. A super hero wouldn't be in any real danger to rush into a burning building to help people trapped inside get out; the Good Samaritan risks smoke inhalation, burns, and death. A super hero would be able to use super powers to gain limitless wealth if she assists financially; a Good Samaritan may struggle to make their own ends meet. A super hero is immediately seen as heroic and yet sometimes the efforts of Good Samaritan's are misjudged entirely.

So what drives a Good Samaritan? Moreover, what drives a wary Samaritan? Most of the people I know who act as Good Samaritans were taught the story of the Good Samaritan as a child in Sunday School. Simply put it plays some part in their Christian ethos. They learned this kind of altruism as children and it's remained with them throughout their lifetimes. For others who are not of the Christian faith, they've learned it in some of the religious teachings they received as children and it too has remained with them throughout their lifetimes. For others still who claim no faith indoctrination I find them to be guided by a personal sense being a Good Samaritan, by whatever name they call it, fulfills their own sense of being connected to humanity in a positive way.

For the wary Samaritan, regardless of how he or she has come to embrace the moniker, there's been one or more, perhaps many more, instances where their Good Samaritan efforts didn't work out quite as flawlessly as they did for the original Good Samaritan. After a particularly bad experience or experiences, most have experienced real trials of their soul as they wrestled with whether or not to ever act as a Good Samaritan again. Make no mistake, there are millions who've tried and given up, never to try again. There are millions more who've tried, given up, and become bitter about the whole experience. They're the ones who react negatively to others who behave as Good Samaritans, because of their own negative experience. Of course you've met them; they told you how ridiculous and misguided all your efforts are.

In summary, some people act rarely as Good Samaritans and it becomes an occasional part of their life, despite any toll taken. Some people act as Good Samaritans once or a few times and the toll taken is so high (e.g., injury, financial loss, death, etc.) they never act again in this fashion. Finally, there's the wary Samaritan, who despite being bloodied, perhaps repeatedly, has counted the cost and decided it's worth the toll taken to press on. Wary Samaritans don't do this because they seek fame. They don't do this because they seek fortune. They don't do this because they believe it will somehow save their souls. Wary Samaritans recognizes deep inside that the path of service to others gives solace to those in time of need and constant meaning to their own lives.

Education Of A Wary Samaritan

This afternoon I dropped by my wife's business to pick up some packages I'd had delivered there. As I drove to the front parking lot I noticed a young woman standing in the rear parking lot of the shop, it was obvious she was crying. I admit I paid it only the least attention, since there are often people on the street who are in various states of emotional excitation and I've learned for the most part it passes. I drove by again ten minutes later and the young woman remained in the same spot and remained tearful. When I returned from Costco in about an hour, there she was, still obviously crying.

I drove past her and then thought better of ignoring her again. I backed up and pulled into the rear parking lot and drove to within thirty feet of her since I didn't want to scare her and make a bad situation worse. I rolled down my window and as it came to a stop I asked her if she was okay. Her response was to shake her head yes. I then asked her if there was anything I could do for her. Once again, she managed to shake her head, only this time no! I told her I'd seen her here for nearly an hour and each time I passed she seemed distressed to me. One last time, I asked her if there was anything I could do, and one last time she shook her head no! I went on my way.

Now some of you are wondering why a wary Samaritan like me didn't press harder in trying to find out what the problem was. Part of the education of a wary Samaritan involves many different types of human encounters with many different types of outcomes. I've learned you can press people too hard and you can make people so uncomfortable your presence is more distressing to them than the reason they're crying in the first place. Good Samaritans truly want to do good! Sometimes in order to do good it's necessary to just leave things, people, and situations, alone. This may be harder for us than any type of personal intervention. Overcome the urge and you'll be better for it!

Keep Your Tools Sharp

Bear with me and read the entire piece; you'll see how it fits in a wary Samaritan's life. I've been using personal computers regularly for 35 years this year. Prior to this date, I played with some of the kits from Tandy and Osborne on my way to early Geekdom. You can imagine my surprise this week when I lost a hard drive for the first time in all those years. I've warned everyone I know about this potential computing catastrophe for decades. To my chagrin, only three of my four computers have those automatic external hard drive backups which backup files continuously. Guess which one of the four died. At any rate, I replaced a 640GB HDD (Hard Disk Drive) with a 1TB version, four years newer for $79.

The truth is over the years I've made a buck or two doing the same thing for other people. Twenty years ago I built PCs, installed servers, and ran business networks with dozens of users on a regular basis. But there came a point in time when I had to decide if I wanted to be the PC Guru or the Chief Executive Officer. I placed theoretical education ahead of technical education; I chose to become a scholar practitioner and have never regretted it. I've continued to work on and build my own PCs, but I have to admit if you're away from the hands-on part of computers and their analogs for even a month, you're a dinosaur.

The new HDD install appears to be a roaring success. Now there'll be two or three days of working and alternately reloading programs and files which were only randomly saved on thumb drives, burned onto CDs or one of the three external HDDs I carry around and regularly forget at home or in the office. I say all of this because a lot of the use I get from my PCs is in charitable works related to my efforts to live out being a good Samaritan. It's important on the way to our lofty goals out there in the highways and the hedges we don't forget there are a lot of mundane things which go to make the world a better place. My father would have said you have to keep your tools sharp.

No Good Deed Goes Unpunished

Oscar Wilde is credited with the phrase, "No good deed goes unpunished." My family and friends would tell you they've been hearing this phrase out of me for the last 40 years. It started for me in early adulthood when I decided to behave regularly in a good Samaritan fashion. I soon discovered those efforts sometimes came back to bite me in the posterior. I want to assure you if you take the story of the Good Samaritan literally and you begin to go out of your way to help people, you'll see, or you've already seen, Mr. Wilde was surprisingly accurate.

So what should you do? Do good deeds anyway! Jesus said we should perform our alms in secret and trust in God to see them and to reward us openly at some future time. Even if there's no obvious reward to your good deed, I believe it's good for your soul to care about others. For those who don't believe in any god or any religious system, do good deeds any way! Your reward will be to have made your world a better place, even if it's only for one other person. At the end of the day this should be enough of a reward for any of us.

The Rest Is Up To You

Sometimes you need to establish your credentials before you begin to speak on a topic if you want to be taken seriously. I'll do this so it seems less like I'm an old man ranting and more like an old man who knows a little bit more than the average man on the street about the things of which he writes. Amongst the half-dozen degrees I've earned, there is a master of Science in Management with a concentration in International Development. Consider also I spent several years working in health care clinics as an administrator, with about half of this time being dedicated to Hospice administration. Consequently, statistics related to international issues about terminal illnesses always catch my attention.

I was reading through a financial advisory letter I subscribe to recently when I ran across some information which caused me to pause. It stated matter-of-factly, in South Africa today AIDS is the leading cause of death, with mankind's' old nemesis, Tuberculosis, running a close second. In many South African provinces around thirty-four percent of the pregnant women are infected with HIV; HIV is the virus that causes AIDS. Of that thirty-four percent, only one percent receives the necessary medical treatment to control the virus to prevent spreading HIV to their unborn child. AIDS remains one hundred percent fatal! Of course in wealthy countries we'll keep you on a pharmaceutical cocktail which works to slow the virus down dramatically; you may live a relatively normal life for many years.

The implications of those few statistics above are remarkable, and this is why I'm remarking about them. Consider for a moment the Spanish Flu Pandemic which ravaged the planet from 1918 to 1920 only had a three percent mortality rate. Between 1918 and 1920, somewhere around thirty-three percent of the world's population was infected with the Spanish Flu. This number is almost identical to the HIV infection rates in South Africa among pregnant women. The Spanish Flu Pandemic had enormous societal implications and affected families, communities, and nations for decades to come. Try to imagine what these numbers mean for South Africa and other African nations with similar statistics in the years ahead. How does the social fabric hold up under such a concerted attack? It may not.

What can a would-be Good Samaritan do? Candidly, I don't know what anyone else can or should do. I do know what I've done over the years and it's been to donate to specific efforts targeted at HIV and AIDS. For some who read this, there may be nothing you're inclined to do and doing nothing is okay. I don't think every good Samaritan has to fight in every battle. Just as in the battles we face in our personal lives, you must pick your wary Samaritan battles carefully in order to be effective. Some who read this may want to become more closely involved and may even feel a tug to personally go there to help, and this too is okay. From time to time in this book I'll make you aware of opportunities like this to be a Good Samaritan; the rest is up to you.

Give A Man A Fish

There is an old adage most of us have heard. It goes something along these lines. "Give a man a fish and you feed him for a day. Teach him to fish and you feed him for a lifetime."

I believe there's a lot of wisdom for wary Samaritans contained in those few words. Over the course of a lifetime I've migrated from the position where I donated to every cause or apparently needy person I met, to the place I'm at now, where I'm extremely wary of who are what I assist.

This came about because in some instances I was directly taken advantage of by individuals claiming needs which didn't exist. In other instances it was the realization some charities I'd donated to were not very good stewards at being both effective and efficient with my donations.

You see, even though I know there are a lot of con artists out there trying to utilize our compassion against us, there are also truly hungry homeless people and there are truly effective and efficient charities which deserve our support. The task is to identify the good ones and avoid the bad ones. This is not as easy to do as it sounds.

I've been at this steadily for four decades and even today I still realize once in a while I've been stung. From time to time I glance at a newspaper, magazine, or eMagazine and see an expose on some charitable group I've supported. Sometimes I still see the hungry and homeless guy I reached out to driving around later in a brand new pickup truck.

Good organizations can falter. Good people can go bad. I've seen it first hand during the 25 years I worked for churches and other not for profit organizations. I held 'C' level positions with two different not for profit organizations with gross incomes of approximately $10,000,000 year. Those kinds of incomes place them in the top 20% of 'not for profits' in the nation. So even though I've worked with not for profits which took in $5000 or less a year, I've also worked for those with a paid staff of 150+ and needed to pull in nearly $1,000,000 a month to keep the doors open.

The constant chase for charity dollars can skew the thinking of leadership and entire boards of directors. The constant exposure to large sums of money, wealthy contributors, and lavish lifestyles can cause leaders to feel a false sense of 'entitlement' to the finer things in life. These are sad truths, but they're truths which each of us need to beware of as we go along the way.

Being a wary Samaritan takes much more effort than being a clueless Good Samaritan. It means you can't just idly hand a dollar to every hungry and homeless guy at the stop sign on the freeway off-ramp. It means you still need to investigate the charity which one of your favorite celebrities is promoting on late night television.

As far as day-to-day acts of charity with strangers goes, I think more and more people are aware of how many of them are scams to provide a tax-free cash income, get money for drugs or alcohol, or to supplement what the professional beggar already receives in some form of government assistance.

I recommend to you a group called Charity Navigator which works constantly to check out charities around the country to see how effective and efficient they actually are with all those dollars charities take in. They won't have records on every charity, but they'll have records on thousands of them. You can access their site at www.charitynavigator.org

I also recommend getting to know what resources are available in your own community to provide food, clothing, shelter, jobs or job training, medical care, and mental health care to those who are truly in need. I know this requires more than parting with a dollar, but it's also more efficient and effective on a personal level.

Just because there's evil in the world and con artists proliferate, don't stop being a Good Samaritan. There's been evil in our world since the beginning of our history and there'll be evil in our world as long as men walk the earth. It's precisely because of this fact the world desperately needs wary Samaritans to be active, diligent in their well doing, and aware of the dangers which exist.

I've Seen The Sausage Made

It happened again today. I first noticed it more than two years ago, but it catches my attention more and more each time I see it occur. I keep telling myself it's just the way things are nowadays, but even then I can't help but feel it's not right. I'm certain it portends some bad things for the social fabric in the decades ahead, and I can only hope if it can't be changed I won't have to live to see it become the norm. There are breaks in the behaviors which mark us as human which seem to grow larger each day.

What am I talking about? I'm talking about watching a young couple come into a restaurant, sit down at a table, and immediately pull out their electronic gadgets and begin to talk or text with some other person. At least I assume it's some other person, perhaps they're communicating with one another and I just don't get it. Whatever happened to people conversing face to face with their dinner companions? Have we so neglected the art of conversation to such degree we've lost it entirely? Is human interaction to be permanently reduced to 140 characters or less?

It's not just in eateries or other casual interactions; I saw problems with this in both for-profit and not-for-profit organizations when I was a COO and even more so later when I was a CEO. I found if you have eight or nine direct reports and your direct reports in turn have a similar or larger number of direct reports, you can become trapped at your desk just trying to respond to the 200+ emails you will invariably get in a single day. You'll 'communicate' with folks down hall and folks in the Washington,

DC office with the same degree of insularity, despite the fact one is only 15 feet away, while the other is 1,500 miles away.

I eventually learned in order to follow the old Hewlett-Packard concept of management by walking around, you have to refuse to go and settle into your desk in the morning or you'll never get away from your tether. Relationships take maintenance, and you're in grave danger of becoming known to your co-workers only through your memos and emails. After a while you aren't flesh and blood at all, you're disembodied bits and bytes rolling across some type of screen or through an earpiece. In these situations, humanity is sacrificed and the magic of human synergy in organizations can be lost entirely.

One of the appeals to me about the story of the Good Samaritan is he was out amongst people, living his regular life, going about his appointed business, yet fully ready to engage with other human beings as the need arose. Contrast this to so many Holy Men and Holy Women in these times who are fully insulated from the rough and tumble of life. I know Pastors who have full security teams, as well as member-servants who essentially wait on them hand and foot. If we're to take Jesus' story seriously, he seems to be holding this lone man out there in the thick of it, meeting and conversing with people face-to-face as being some sort of an exemplar. We'd do well to emulate his example.

Here Am I, Send Me

I'd say the most encouraging development I've seen in Good Samaritanism over the past forty years is the rise of regular folks taking on the role of short-term to medium-term involvement in reaching out to the needy in either our inner cities or foreign locales, by personally going there and pitching in. When I was a kid, we were regaled with stories from professional Foreign Missionaries, professional Home Missionaries, or the Peace Corp members who had gone to foreign countries or America's inner cities to lend a helping hand to the less fortunate.

Today I know many regular people with no specialized training other than their existing skill set who have gone on short-term efforts as teachers, pilots, carpenters, plumbers, agronomists, stone masons, electricians, accountants, printers, physicians, dentists, nurses, health educators, well drillers, mechanics, and support staff (i.e., someone has to feed and take care of the volunteers). Sometimes they're only there for a few days, in other instances they may stay an entire year. Some of them are retired and dreamed of this for a lifetime, but others are people still in the workforce who take their own vacation time and money and volunteer it for a worthy cause.

So if you're considering doing something of this sort either during your working career or after you retire, you should begin to research the possibilities right now. Whether you're closely associated with some type of a fraternal order or an organized religious group, my guess is they'll know of opportunities both at home and abroad. Your local, state, and federal governments all have a need for volunteers to help in many places and with a varied assortment of skill sets. The possibilities are nearly limitless and the needs have never been greater. Even if you're a wary Samaritan, the planet and its inhabitants need you if you've got some time to spare.

Value Of Authenticity

I wonder a lot in recent years about how much social media actually brings people together versus how much it just makes those who use it expert at managing their posted image. I'm certainly not immune from this and do my best to make posts which are articulate and entertaining so my friends on Facebook and other similar cyber locales will continue to think I'm urbane and witty.

What every wary Samaritan might want to guard against is managing our cyber persona so well we become bland and irrelevant to real human beings. No one I know or have ever met in the real world has a perfect life. When I routinely see these perfect lives depicted in cyberspace, I begin to take them with a grain of salt. I encounter folks regularly who haven't posted or tweeted an original fact, idea, or insight in years.

This leaves me wondering how people are really doing. I don't believe the façade and I worry about the lack of reality. I've lived one of those warts and all lives where my bad moments have gotten far more ink than my good ones. I've chosen to live in a transparent way so people who might otherwise think "Wow! What a wonderful life he has," don't become discouraged in their own lives. All of us have realities in our day-to-day living which cause us to be far less than perfect.

We already have a surfeit of inauthentic lives being depicted by some singers, actors, writers, celebrities, preachers, and politicians; note I said some. Consider the value to others in being authentic and don't allow yourself to become a purveyor of homogeneous nothingness. The whole world needs to see real people living and overcoming personal and professional challenges before their eyes.

Forget The Lone Ranger Approach
Periodically I'll encounter a person who'll glowingly recount to me their Good Samaritanly efforts. To hear them tell it, they did

it all on their own. I've been blessed in my life to be a part of some really great efforts to make the world a better place, and truth be told I can't recall a single instance where I could take credit for the entire effort, even when others ascribed it to me. I'm reminded regularly of people who helped me a great deal when I was a boy and made a positive difference in the man I am today. If each of us searches our hearts hard enough, we'll know with certainty that none of us does this alone.

What's In It for Me

If you're going to be a Good Samaritan, it does not occur because you're too dense to figure out it will be 'costly', it occurs because having done the math, and seeing the possible negative outcomes, you still press ahead because there's such a potential positive in helping others.

I believe all of the folks, who upon seeing a man's body laying at the side of the road and having made a point of passing along to the other side, did so because they'd done the math and decided not to get involved. That's a natural reaction to such a repulsive and potentially dangerous event.

I'm not saying take no thought about yourself or your well-being (feel free to ignore what Jesus said); each of us will naturally want to protect his or her own life. A wary Samaritan is no fool! A wary Samaritan has likely been burned before, perhaps burned many times, and yet knows deep down inside doing the right thing, is the right thing to do.

I suspect there'll always be more people turning their head and walking on by than there will be people who go onto the roadside and become involved in the nasty business of life. It takes a special set of eyes to look onto one of life's calamities and recognize a place and time where one needs to step in, instead of stepping away.

CHAPTER 2

A Wary Samaritan's Prayer

Lord, as I go about my day today, bring me into contact with the people you want me to meet. Allow me to be perceptive enough to recognize you brought them my way. Give me the wisdom to know what to do or not to do, what to say or not to say, and what to offer or not to offer... Amen

Learning And Moving On

You don't have to hand out cash to be a good Samaritan, yet some folks feel it's the only thing they can do. Regardless of the method you choose to help people, always be wary. I know this sounds cynical, but I want you to keep a good heart for a lifetime and not become embittered by negative fallout from your good deeds. A businessman friend recounted to me recently how he tries to give work to contractors who are having a tough time of it; I knew where his story was headed.

He went on to share how he's become disenchanted with this approach, since these people and their families are often in dire straits and in order to help them immediately he tries to prepay for the work. The end result is that frequently once they receive the money, they start the project and then either never comes back, or it takes months of chasing, wheedling, and cajoling to get them to honor their side of the exchange by completing the work. Think of this as the feed-me chase-me approach.

Here's how to handle this in your future. Most states have laws which limit such prepayments. Why not just make a legal/reasonable deposit and then make progress payments as each phase or day is completed. Good Samaritans tend to lead with their heart. This immediately puts us at a disadvantage if we encounter someone with less than noble motives. Just because they're broke and struggling doesn't mean they're scrupulously honest. Hey, maybe that's why they're broke and struggling.

Years ago a church friend who was a material supplier asked me to pay for an entire project up front because, "Brother... my cash flow is slow right now and I was hoping you could help me out." I did it to help him out, but within two weeks I got a letter from his attorney saying he'd made a bankruptcy filing. Within a month of the 1st letter I got a 2nd letter telling me the bankruptcy was total and there were no assets. I was heartsick and out a significant amount of money.

I realized later he'd likely been pondering bankruptcy by the time he spoke with me. It turned out he'd hit several of his church friends in the same manner. Once the bankruptcy was final, he left the church crowd behind. Whether out of shame or by design, I can't say. But it was a bitter pill for each of us who'd advanced him money to swallow as our good had been turned against us as evil and our own businesses and families were negatively affected by his deceit.

For a while I vowed I'd learned my lesson and would never trust anyone again. Of course this wore off in time as I realized never trusting anyone again wasn't going to be a livable solution without becoming distant and bitter. Over the years I've learned that to be a wary Samaritan, at times I'd have to stay engaged and simultaneously NOT just hand over money out of sympathy. So today I still help other people when I can, but I'm much wiser about how I do it. Doing good works doesn't require throwing all caution to the wind!

You Don't Have To Be A Boy Scout

When I was young I enjoyed Scouting. For those of you who don't recall hearing the term, it means I was a member of the Boy Scouts of America. I joined up when I was almost eight years old and was active for six years. There were two key tenets taught to me in those days which have remained with me continuously over the years: "Be Prepared" and "Do a Good Deed Daily." At first I had to consciously remind myself about both of them, but as the years went by they became a part of the man I grew to be. They're both such an integral part of me now I'm only aware I'm doing one or the other if I'm questioned or reminded about my actions. Such is the transformative power of the habits we develop in childhood.

Scouting is no longer as popular or widespread as it was when I was a boy, but I think we can still hang onto those old school ideas. Being prepared is another issue for another day, but doing good deeds is here and now. The magical thing I learned about doing good deeds is they ripple across the pond of our lives and their waves wash up upon our shores, sometimes months, years, or even decades later. We often forget this truth and feel as if we may have done a foolish thing by trying to do some good deed.

I think it's why we've been reminded in the scripture if we don't allow ourselves to grow weary in our well-doing, we'll eventually enjoy a harvest from the seeds of goodness and kindness we've planted through the years.

Recharging Your Soul

As I write this, in some parts of the nation the weather is beginning to improve with snow melting and even some greenery starting to peek through. This week, to help balance out some of those negatives you'll undoubtedly encounter, take a few minutes each day to admire the good things God has placed in the world around you. When I discipline myself to seek out and meditate upon the good and lovely things in our world, it makes it easier to later encounter some of the bad and ugly things in our world and not become depressed by them.

I recall from a reading in grad school that scientist and educator George Washington Carver encouraged the poor of the Southern United States to replant wildflowers around their homes, which they could find growing wild in the fields and woods. He felt by placing the beautiful flowering plants near the doors of their homes, each day they saw some of God's handiwork and were reminded life is not all dreariness and sorrow. In the same manner, I believe if we take time to find some beauty each day, it empowers us and later helps take the sting out of life's uglier moments.

Where Nobody Knows Your Name

The real people you and I are emerge when we're alone and no one else can see or hear us. The same can be said for Good Samaritanism. It's one thing to perform a good work where the beneficiary and/or others (e.g., family, friends, neighbors, church, IRS, etc.) are aware of what you've done. It's another matter altogether to perform a good work which only you and God will ever know about. As a wary Samaritan I've come to suspect there are far more of these hidden opportunities which arise than there are open and obvious ones.

The first Good Samaritan appears to have been a stranger passing along the road when he happened upon the victim of a violent physical attack and robbery. He doesn't appear to have been personally acquainted with the victim and there's no record of whether or not the victim was even conscious enough to recognize or thank his benefactor. We don't know what specific congregation in Samaria he's affiliated with or if he's even a particularly religious member of the Samaritan community. To my knowledge no given name is ever applied to the Good Samaritan. Consequently, he becomes a type of everyman who ever performed a good work.

What do we know about him? Well, we know he intervened with a stranger when others who may well have known the stranger did not. We know at least one member of the secular community went out of his way to ignore the victim. We know at least one member of the religious establishment went out of his way to ignore the victim. We know the Samaritan interrupted his own life to become actively involved in the personal hardship of another. We know he took the time to secure the victim's welfare AND used his own money to do so. We know several other facts which I won't mention here, but we don't know his name.

One of my favorite sayings has been attributed to the late United States President Ronald Reagan. "There is no limit to the amount of good you can do if you don't care who gets the credit."

On the journey of a wary Samaritan it's a red-letter day when you know in your heart you truly don't care anymore who gets the credit. I'm not saying it isn't nice to be recognized and credited, because it is! Recognize that when you can be just as happy with the overall outcome and nobody even suspects you were the architect or one of the facilitators of a good work, you've passed a critical turning point in your soul.

Reading The Obituaries

For at least 40 years I've read the obituaries in *The Bakersfield Californian* the first thing each morning. Years ago it was a physical newspaper; today it's an electronic edition. The practical aspect of the practice remains to be certain I'm not listed among the deceased and then waste my entire day pretending I'm still alive. Further, it lets me know if any old friends have died or if members of their family have passed on and attendance at a memorial, a sympathy card, or flowers are called for. But in all truthfulness I also read those obituaries and compare my life to those lives which are now finished.

I wonder about how old they were. I wonder what they died from. I wonder where they were from and where they lived during the course of their life. I wonder where they went to school. I wonder if they were married, divorced, or single. I note their family, or lack thereof. I look at any indication of some spiritual path they followed. I look at their career. I look at their choice of how they wished their remains handled (i.e., burial, cremation, cryogenic preservation, etc.). Finally, I'm interested in what they did as an avocation.

You can tell a great deal about people by the things they did away from their jobs, the things which gave them an outlet and enjoyment. There are those who show a strong good Samaritan streak and there are others, who it seems clear, were self-obsessed. There are others still, whose lives show a healthy mix of the two. I'm surprised at how often I see obituaries for folks from previous generations who seem to have been conditioned to giving and gave of themselves right to the end. Some go beyond this and donate their bodies to medical science.

The only judgment I ever try to pass while reading these obituaries is upon me. How do I measure up? What would my obituary look like if today were my last day? Over the years, I've seen the obituaries of some truly amazing human beings; most of them were not famous. The works they did and the lives they affected were directly in their path; people and situations they'd come in contact with across a lifetime. Each of us is afforded the opportunity to touch our world. What we do with it may only be noted at the time of our passing.

Caveat Emptor – Good Samaritan Beware

Wary Samaritans are painfully aware of the meaning of *caveat emptor*. I want to add an area where I think more of us need to be wary buyers. I was reading an online article the other day on shortages of natural resources around the world and in the course of the article I began to think, "...this is fantastic." Now I don't mean fantastic in the way most people use it these days where it indicates something we regard as great or phenomenal. I mean fantastic in the sense the information offered began to border on fantasy. You see, I'm prejudiced in this particular area because a great deal of my research for my master's degree was in the field being touted. So when what I read in popular literature doesn't match what I read in scientific literature, I balk.

I need to point out in conducting graduate research you have to credit your assertions (claims); you can't just make them up and toss them in as you go along. Any serious author who's ever built a 10-page bibliography to support a thesis of any sort knows exactly what I'm talking about. Not only would your reviewers question such obvious absences of attribution, your peers would laugh you out of the field for writing fiction rather than research. Yet when it comes to Internet writing, unsupported facts are thrown about like beads at Mardi gras. Unfortunately, if you show us something which titillates us, we'll often abandon all criticality and reason. I see this occurring at an alarming rate in popular culture. It's a trend which doesn't bode well for actual supported facts.

It's often lamented we live in an age where people want to be entertained and if you want to hold an audience, the more entertaining you are the better. I understand this and know from thousands of hours of public speaking if you don't have the ability to hold your audience with your mastery of the facts, you can always resort to drama, comedy, tragedy, fashion, or the daily news to hold their attention. However, when this effort to gain and hold an audience's attention begins propagandizing us to shape national and/or international policy through carefully scripted emotional appeals (which may or may not be based on fact) the entertainment value is too much and the factual value is too little!

So the next time you begin to read some kind of an appeal, whether they're vying for your dollars, your mind, your soul, your body, your vote, or all of the above, be a wary Samaritan. I've found with regard to articles where they offer an email at the end so you can contact the writer to request supporting data for their assertions, or references supporting their work, you either never hear back from these folks or you hear back the supporting evidence is all anecdotal. In simplest terms this means it's from an observation or word of mouth rather than critically verified facts. It's a mistake to base our good works on the assertions of an author whose hyperbole may cover a hidden agenda.

A lot of the facts associated with the work of a wary Samaritan are boring and tedious. Most of life is actually mundane and only on a reality television show can the average day-to-day be turned into rollicking entertainment. The headline *"Millions Killed by Winged Death"* will certainly garner more reads than the headline, *"Mosquito Bites Continue to Be a Major Health Problem."* I accept the fact a writer or speaker must first gain our attention in order to convey a message. What you and I can't and shouldn't accept is a distortion of the facts or an outright fabrication of the facts in order to get people to react in a way the author desires. The sooner every would-be Good Samaritan embraces and practices this critical mindset, the sooner speculators and charlatans will lose their ability to thrive and multiply.

What's Your Hidden Talent

Sharing your knowledge is a powerful way to make a difference in the world. Recently I watched an older neighbor share his knowledge of how to set up and plant a garden with a younger neighbor. This good work resonates on so many levels it's hard to hone in on just one. This act of giving of one's self cements a relationship with the younger neighbor, simultaneously building community. It helps this young neighbor provide a healthier and less expensive source of vegetables for the family. It passes along a skill which will be valuable to the young neighbor and perhaps to the young neighbor's offspring. So, the next time you think your life skills have no value, think again.

No matter what it is you know there's someone closer than you think who doesn't know what you know and would benefit from your knowledge. I deeply value the people on YouTube® who take the time to offer videos of their skills. Even when they put up something I think I already I know, I find I will invariably learn some new element of some task I figured I'd mastered years ago. People around us need to learn all sorts of things to improve the quality of their lives. Knowing and sharing how to paint a bathroom, how to cook a roast, how to mend a damaged window screen, or how to replace a piston in an old engine, all have the ability to change lives for the better.

This doesn't mean you should rush out and buy a new Sony video camera and start posting your every moment on YouTube®. It does mean we should all be aware of what's going on near at hand and who we regularly encounter that would benefit from something we know and are currently taking the 'knowing' for granted. I'm not suggesting you force yourself on people. I'm suggesting you let people know if you have a skill set you think they might need or benefit from and then allow them to either rise to the bait or swim on by. Make the offer and then allow the offeree to decide if they're buying or rejecting your offer. Don't let your feelings get in the way and be loving in either instance.

The "It Takes A Village" Good Samaritan

In other writings I warned against the dangers of becoming a Lone Ranger Samaritan. Today I'd like to warn against the other extreme, the It Takes a Village Samaritan. The Lone Ranger Samaritan tends to always insist on exercising their Samaritanism by working alone. His or her counterpart, the It Takes a Village Samaritan, is unable to do anything unless they can get a crowd of people to join them or at least watch them. I don't think either approach is healthy for a steady diet. There are moments of opportunity in life where we must work within groups, for any number of reasons. There are other moments of opportunity in life which present themselves where there's either no one else able or willing to help or other Wary Samaritans on site are too wary or flatly refuse to help at all.

The original Good Samaritan appears to have acted entirely on his own. This wasn't because he necessarily wanted to act alone; it was because he had too. If we stand by waiting for back up, back up may never arrive. If we stand by waiting for someone else to take the lead, the critical moment of need may be permanently lost. I hate to raise this issue in an increasingly secular and cynical age, but what's the 'still small voice' in your heart saying you should do? This voice often defies logic. This voice often asks me to put myself out there. I don't always like what this voice has to say. I suspect those of you who hear this particular voice (as opposed to the many voices in some heads) has heard some of the same uncomfortable promptings which I have.

Think of how many times in history God's called upon an unlikely hero to act alone. The reason we know their names and regard them as heroic is because they responded affirmatively to God's voice when the crowd didn't. There were millions of others who have gone unknown because they ignored God's voice, passed by on the other side of the road, and went about their own business. Let me reiterate that I do understand there are times when only a village will do. Far more often than not, there won't be a village available. Recently I administered first-aid to a young boy who'd been seriously injured by a hit and run driver. The accident occurred in front of my home, but I didn't know the child or speak his language well. I looked around at the village which had gathered to observe and realized if I didn't act, none of them were going to. They were busy recording the event on their smart phones. He made it to the ambulance and the hospital okay with some broken bones, a cracked skull, and a concussion. About two weeks later I saw him out in his yard wearing one of those halo contraptions and a year later he has some bad head scars, but appears otherwise normal.

Our world right now is in desperate need of people who can work in groups when the group is available and who can and will work alone when the group disappears. If only we could ask the first Good Samaritan about his experience. Blood scares people, crime scares people, getting dirty scares people, being late for an appointment scares people, and spending their own money to help someone in need scares people. Some people must have a crowd present to perform. I call those folks performer Samaritans. Yet it's been my experience when it comes to performing good deeds, there are a lot of folks who are performer Samaritans in the sense they only act when their efforts are observed. I'll go further and assert there are people who go out of their way to be credited for good works they didn't do. Be a Good Samaritan… crowd or no crowd.

Encouraging The Wary Samaritans

I like to make routine efforts to be an encourager and an encouragement to other wary Samaritans; this can be done either by admonition or by example. Sometimes this comes in the form of just minding my own business and not letting anyone else know I know them. Then there are times when people aren't afraid to admit we're acquainted and I can be more actively involved in their efforts. It may mean I bring the contents of the closets I've just cleaned out to the local animal shelter thrift shop. It may mean I go by the dollar store and pick up a bunch of toiletries to support a wary Samaritan making up 'personal bags' for the local homeless shelter. It may mean I bring a bag of groceries and drop them off at the Teen Challenge Men's or Women's Home. It may mean I go by Catholic Charities with a back seat full of boxed cereals I found on sale at Big Lots®.

It's been said "You can't live off of praise." I'd agree! Conversely, there's no indication we shouldn't praise other's efforts at all or we shouldn't demonstrate our appreciation of what they're doing by supporting their good works. Taking advantage of any of these opportunities to support another wary Samaritan's efforts multiplies our own giving. How so you might ask? Well, first we're directly supporting the effort at hand (e.g., feeding the hungry, caring for the homeless, caring for neglected animals, providing a breakfast to kids who might not otherwise have one, etc.). Secondly, and just as importantly, we tangibly signal the wary Samaritan or Samaritans who are taking the lead in the effort that we believe in them and we're willing to show it in ways others can see.

Rescuing Ourselves

As odd as this may seem, befriending the friendless can be a powerful expression of faith for a wary Samaritan. This realization occurred to me over the Easter Holiday while watching a holiday gathering at my youngest daughter's home and realizing many of the people there were either new to the area, were local but lacked local contacts, or perhaps were at an age when many of their family and friends had already passed on. My daughter Rachel and her husband Dave have made an effort for years to reach out to people who are new to the Hollywood area, having once been new there themselves and learned first-hand what a lonely place it can be.

The result of these kinds of random gatherings is always an interesting mix of young and old, celebrity and unknown, hip and not so hip. I've never asked but I'm certain there've been times when one of the invitees did not turn out to be a stellar guest. Occasionally, someone drinks too much, talks too loud, or even falls asleep at the table. However, I can't say these events are boring and I look forward to attending them when time allows. Somehow over the years many of these folks have become friends and are now fixtures in their lives and no longer strangers. I've come to know them; I know their stories, and I know their victories and defeats.

I'm at an age where many of my friends complain about the dull routine of their lives. This transpires because as we age and grow comfortable on multiple levels with our daily existence, we rarely want to risk the potential cost of new relationships. New relationships are messy and expensive on several levels. I've come to realize sometimes the very thing a wary Samaritan needs in order to revitalize his or her life is to risk finding out who the man or woman lying on the roadside actually is. Anonymously sending a check to some mega-ministry or celebrity charity, welcome as it no doubt is, never forces us to get our hands dirty. By rescuing the life in the ditch we may in fact be enriching and saving our own.

Unsung Heroes And Heroines

It's always a pleasant surprise to get acquainted with some older person and discover they led a heretofore unrecognized remarkable life. I've experienced this several times in becoming acquainted with elderly men and women, who upon first encounter seemed quite unremarkable. It happens less often these days, but I used to regularly encounter men and women who'd lived through and participated in World War II. Reporter Tom Brokaw called them *The Greatest Generation* and he may well be correct in my estimation. These men and women tended to be matter of fact and totally unassuming about the heroic lives they'd led and the incredible work they did. Even then, to gain a small bit of insight from them often took verbally pulling it, piece by piece.

What I learned from this is if we care enough to ask, there are people all around us who deserve recognition and never ask for it. This seems odd to me because we're at a time when I feel we could use all the positive role models and outright heroes and heroines we can find. The odd part is there are likely men and women in our own families, neighborhoods, or communities who have accomplished remarkable goals or performed heroic feats which have gone completely unnoticed. I recall thirty-five years back looking through a box full of medals of a man I thought I knew and coming across a Silver Star with two oak leaf clusters. When I held it up and inquired, he was dismissive about my calling him a hero and immediately changed the topic. He'd earned them as an infantryman in combat.

My guess is all around us are people who've lived lives which are noteworthy, which also go entirely unnoticed. Is it possible sometimes the healing work of a wary Samaritan is to find, recognize, and honor those unsung heroes and heroines all around us? At any point in history there are women and men who've been pioneers, leaders, and world changers. But as time marches on their exploits are quickly forgotten and eventually their light slowly fades, they die, and the parade of life moves on. Part of being a wary Samaritan is living in community. It doesn't detract from any of us to search for and highlight the best of other people's lives within the community. I'd suggest we start with our own families and work out from there. There may well be a hero or heroine going unnoticed nearby.

Do As I Do, Not As I Say
Why is it many people who send email, tweets, text, or posts about great people and their noble causes seem to lack any personal desire to emulate those persons? I see this evidenced by what the old-timers would've called a lack of works. Some of the most annoying and least involved people I know send information and/or quotations about/from the Dali Lama, Jesus, Buddha, Mother Teresa, Physicians Without Borders, St. Francis, and Martin Luther King, Jr. This particular writing exercise of mine doesn't focus on wary Reporters.

Call me a wary Samaritan, but I only take them seriously when people send me information about causes they're personally involved in. I'm puzzled when people who are always advising others on what Good Samaritanly acts they should undertake, have actually spent their own lives blissfully uninvolved! There's no personal cost to be disengaged. Many unsung Good Samaritans have been busy doing for decades and plan to be busy doing until they die. Why not go do it yourself, then send the rest of us a first person account of your experiences? I know this may sound mean and it's not intended to be, but a little first-person report once in a while would re-establish credibility.

Rolling With The Punches
I'm old enough I'm no longer surprised when at some point after I've made an effort to behave as a Good Samaritan, I receive one or more stinging criticisms. At this point I think I've heard them all, but I never say never in these instances because people

continue to surprise me. Tonight I received an angry email from a lady I've known for 40 years, because in the course of trying to honor a group of people, I'd failed to be aware of two of her family members who should have been recognized and weren't listed on the announcement I put on Facebook®.

Never mind that I'd solicited this information on five different Facebook pages, the local media, mass snail mailings, and even a series of mass emails over six months; this woman felt certain I'd personally singled out her loved ones for exclusion. I learned years ago to never send the first email I write in response to attacks like this. It's better to absorb the venom and then do your best to dissipate it through some combination of prayer and silent blasphemies than to immediately respond in kind. By the second or third draft, logic has regained control, I have become conciliatory, and I'm searching for common ground.

Wary Samaritans are wary with good cause. However, you'll notice I didn't entitle this book Reflections of an Angry Samaritan, Cynical Samaritan, or Vengeful Samaritan. Instead, I wanted to emphasize in getting burned we have to work hard not to become angry, cynical, scarred, bitter, or vengeful. I've no idea whether I've gained a sister out of this or if I've just created a new enemy. What I do know is if you and I keep our hearts in the right place, the efforts we make will abound to good, regardless of the handful of people who'll always be unhappy...

CHAPTER 3

Gary Brown

As I write this I'm allowing a twenty-year old to help me in some of my electrical work. Despite my age and associated health conditions slowing me down, I can still work faster and accomplish more alone than I can with him helping. So, why don't I just tell him to move along?

When I was a young man an older man graciously took me under his wing and taught me some basic skills. Those skills paved the way for me to one day move from being a mechanic's helper, to being a welder, to being a contractor, and eventually to being able to earn a doctorate. That man's name was Gary Brown. Gary's been dead for many years now.

I look back on the time when I was nineteen and understand now how for the better part of a year Gary carried me when he didn't have any obligation to do so. Every day at work he patiently taught me, and more than forty years later I can't ever recall Gary raising his voice when I messed up; and I did mess up.

Now, it's this wary Samaritan's turn to carry someone else.

Look Before You Leap

Not all efforts to be a Good Samaritan end well. I think about this truth each time I read the story of the Good Samaritan in the New Testament and it appears to end so well. I know that's not what anybody wants to hear, but for those of you who've been at this for a while, you're a wary Samaritan because not all your efforts have ended well. As if you'd need more proof, why do you think states have adopted the so-called Good Samaritan Laws? As I recall, it was because people had become reluctant to try and help the woman on the roadside because she was likely to turn around and sue them once she did recover. Or, if she didn't recover, her family came after the would-be Good Samaritan for wrongful death or some other nightmarish tort theory.

I know it will sound like lyrics from some sad country song, but in the course of becoming a wary Samaritan you'll see both the very best and the very worst in human behavior. Over the years wary Samaritans have been lied to, lied about, threatened, cheated, beaten, raped, burglarized, robbed, sued, tortured, and even murdered in the course of trying to live out this Gospel truth. In my own case, I haven't been raped, sued, or murdered in the course of my efforts, but I can easily identify with the rest of the list. It boils down to vulnerability! In order to truly be out there for the people who need a wary Samaritan most, you'll find yourself in dicey situations which you may not always have taken the time to clear-headedly assess before you jumped in. STOP!

Here's my advice. Don't stop reaching out. Do lead with your head and your heart, not just your heart. You're a grown person and you've been around. Take off your blinders before you head for the person in the ditch. Is it a set up? Is she really hurt? Are you capable of direct intervention or is your very best and wisest effort to dial 911? I know there's an urge to act instantly sometimes, which we should fight with all our might to avoid. One of the things I value about my years in healthcare was to have developed the ability to stay rational in the face of life and death decisions. Consequently, I now urge other similarly action-oriented wary Samaritans to slow down and look things over for as long as you safely can, before making the decision as to how, or even if you'll become involved.

Starve A Dozen

I'm of the opinion, given limited resources, it's better to do a good job of feeding one hungry person than to do a terrible job of feeding a dozen hungry persons. I know how cold and un-Christ like this sounds to many who'll read this, but only in the first instance do you have the opportunity to gain a fully fed ally to assist you in multiplying your initial and ongoing effort. The two of you in turn may now help two others, and so on. Whereas in the second instance, you've now assumed responsibility for watching a dozen people slowly starve to death. You'll initially feel better about yourself, but this feeling won't last long as they die before your eyes.

In these cases under the second scenario, your agonized pleas to others will grow louder and shriller. But in the end the outcome is still a dozen have starved to death. Some of the charities which I watch regularly seem to always take the route of starving a dozen rather than saving one at a time. Of course, you don't get much publicity by changing the world one person at a time. It doesn't generate many photo opportunities. No one hands out humanitarian awards to the 'one person at a time' crowd. I suppose we each must decide what our real goal is and then pursue it. Usually, I'm better if I'm focused on the victim in immediately front of me.

What Will the Neighbors Think

When I was a young minister I was assured by older and wiser ministers you couldn't enjoy any ministerial success if you stayed in your hometown. Being the contrarian I am, I ignored such sage advice. In retrospect I might well have been more successful in another place where I was an unknown entity. But there's something to be said for living out your life among people you've known forever. Yes, by leaving I could've distanced myself from past family drama and my own youthful mistakes. I could've completely recreated myself and no one would've been the wiser.

For some ministers I've known this worked well and I don't begrudge them their choices. In short, the path I took is the same one most people who aren't going into public ministry take, they grew where they were planted and made the best of it. Many became wary Samaritans along the way and still managed to do some good. I've learned you can never really hide from your childhood, your family, or the mistakes you made growing up. The inability to hide is even truer in these times of widespread social media. However, you can embrace your life, warts and all, and still find success at all levels if you'll own your victories as well as your defeats and move along with integrity.

Sometimes The Victim Won't Cooperate

In case you've missed this lesson on the road to your own wary Samaritanism, sometimes the victim won't cooperate. Some victims feel they deserved to be robbed, beaten, and left for dead. Some victims are tired of resisting attack and just give into it. Some victims would rather resist you than be rescued by you or anyone else. Some victims have actually begun to find comfort in the familiar surroundings of the ditch and the associated victimization. You my friend have to be able to look in their eyes and recognize when the moment comes when you must walk away or perish there beside them.

Neighborhood Good Samaritan

If there ever was a time in American history when we needed a renewed sense of community, it's the time we live in now. As an eleven year old boy back in 1965, I knew two thirds of the people who lived in my neighborhood and they knew me. Fast forward to 2015, a mere 50 years later and though I still live in the same house, try as I might I'd guess I only know about one tenth of them. Not only have the demographics of my neighborhood changed over fifty years, people have too. We're definitely warier of others than we were back then, and we're wary with good reason. It seems to this observer the values of those times have given way to a near complete lack of values in this time.

I suppose you and I could just give in to the urge to become cynical in this cynical age, but it would be better for all of us if you and I don't. The people who've lived through Hurricane Katrina, Superstorm Sandy, and any other major natural disaster are relearning how much members of a community need one another. One of the quickest ways to get to know a neighbor is to be ready to reach out to them in those moments in life we all experience where we need a helping hand of one sort or another. So this week, while you're trying hard to live out your faith by your works, look among your unmet neighbors to see if one of them has a visible need which could be met by a wary Samaritan.

Teach Your Children Well

Teaching our children and our grandchildren the important lessons demonstrated by The Good Samaritan assures us there'll be concern and compassion for the less fortunate in future generations. Conversely, if we teach them they're the center of their own universe, they'll grow up to be shallow, inconsiderate, and compassionless men and women. I've met more than one parent or grandparent who made the mistake of raising the latter kind of child or grandchild. When the parents or grandparents grew old, they were shocked to find themselves the victims of their own poor parenting and/or grand parenting.

Wary But Willing
Do you ever wonder what was going through the minds of the people that moved on down the highway past the victim described in the story of The Good Samaritan? By and far they were a good cross-section of the citizenry and based on their beliefs and professions they should've been among the first to offer to lend a hand. Instead, I suspect they began to almost immediately arm themselves psychologically so they could justify leaving this man to his own devices; you and I have both done the same at times.

So, whenever we indict those who walked on, we're also indicting our own bad behavior. I'm fairly certain God doesn't feel like you or I have a duty to stop at every car accident, crop failure, bicycle wreck, or faulty barn raising. I'm also fairly certain God does feel you and I have a duty to stop at some of them. Be honest, you know which ones they are just as I do. I claim for myself the title wary Samaritan, as do some of you. Let us wary Samaritans then agree to strive to be wary, but also strive to remain willing.

We Won't Be Fooled Again
If you read the news stories some time back about a young lady named Brittany Ozarowski, you know sometimes even the

wariest among us get taken. It seems Ms. Ozarowski had been feigning cancer for two years in order to scam the public and her family out of money for her heroin addiction. During those two years literally dozens of Good Samaritans stepped up to donate what's now estimated to have been more than $200,000 for her cancer-treatment. For some of the donors this event is the tipping point which will turn them into wary Samaritans. But the saddest part is for others among those donors this will be the tipping point which ends any Good Samaritan behavior forever.

What Ozarowski did is both reprehensible and a crime. I recognize she's an addict, but addiction does not excuse this kind of thievery. She hurt both her community and her family as she stole from both groups. In one instance her grandmother sold her home and gave Brittany $100,000 of the proceeds to be used for her cancer-treatments. As a consequence, Brittany Ozarowski is being charged with 24 counts of criminal behavior. My guess is she'll get some time, some rehab, and be ordered to pay back the money. But, the worst outcome of her scam is her behavior has all but assured one day some victim lying on a roadside somewhere will be passed by as one of Brittany Ozarowski's donor-victims refuses to risk ever being scammed again.

Can They Be Trusted

Are you supporting the most insistent doers of good works (charities), or the most deserving doers of good works? Are the folks who constantly hound you for money truly the best place to be sending your money? Are there lesser known and less aggressive charities which might get more bang for your wary Samaritan buck? Some of you ponder these same questions I do and some of you simply open your wallets to the next paid solicitor who dials your number, knocks at your door, or manages to get something into your email or mailbox.

If you're like me you get solicitations by mail, email, and telephone regularly from worthy causes looking for those wary Samaritans out there to lend a helping hand in the form of donations. As mentioned earlier I've worked for some large nonprofits and know all too well fundraising is an ongoing challenge and a matter of organizational life and death. Over the years I've become very cautious about whom I donate to out of fear the money ends up in the wrong hands. By this I mean it either gets squandered on pie-in-the-sky or administrative costs eat up a huge chunk of it and leave little for the actual good work.

Some years back I encountered an organization called Charity Navigator. It was one of the best encounters I've ever had. That's because they're a non-profit which tracks the works of other nonprofits. This helps those of us who are asked to donate from a distance make certain our good works aren't wasted on bloated administrative costs and other questionable expenditures. Charity Navigator has reviews of thousands of nonprofits and they're free on their website. Charity Navigator does accept donations to support their efforts and if you'd like to know more about Charity Navigator or one of your favorite charities, they're at www.charitynavigator.org

Be Wary, Not Heartless

A few years back *The New York Times* ran an article on panhandlers and how much they took in during an average year. People were aghast at the sums which in several cases far exceeded the average income of a working New Yorker. Since then we've heard the same scenario played out over and over again, all across the nation. Many of you, as I do, have horror stories about the abuses you've seen being carried out by the hungry, the homeless, and the down on his luck veteran. Mostly the stories illustrated these fakers have turned out not to be hungry, not to be homeless, and not to be veterans. The variations on these themes are endless and the male and female perpetrators of these hoaxes seem to have an amazing ability to rework these scams endlessly so they can create a new donor appeal each season.

Now before you start sending me hate mail or ugly emails, I do know there are people who are hungry, homeless, and veterans out there on America's streets. I know it because I've worked with groups who reach out to try and turn these lives around and get them off the streets. I can say with definity it's a much more difficult job than just dropping some change in their basket or giving them a sack lunch and telling them "God loves you." Often there are drug or alcohol issues; there are physical health issues; and quite frequently mental health issues which need to be addressed to really be of any help to the truly needy on the streets. The complex nature of the problems is why I suggest you hang onto your change and find real efforts to do more than buy them today's heroin or tonight's beer.

While I've seen a few families out panhandling, it's mostly been single men and women. The true face of homelessness in our country has aimed more toward entire families since the housing bubble burst a few years back. These are the times in which a wary Samaritan should thrive by not being taken in or scammed. Continue to care for the poor and the homeless, but do it responsibly! As hard as it is for some to accept, there are people who choose to live on the streets rather than be bound by the rules of any congregate living arrangement. In my experience this is especially the case with the many who struggle with mental illness and/or addictions. The true tragedy is to see a family on the street only to learn Mom and/or Dad have pulled their kids into their drug, alcohol, or mental illness nightmare.

In my area we have a Homeless Shelter, a Gospel Rescue Mission, a Salvation Army Men's Home, Teen Challenge Women's Home, Teen Challenge Men's Home, Catholic Charities, St. Vincent De Paul, and a handful of other similar projects ran by local nonprofits. Why not find out what it is they or other similar groups are doing in your area and see if they could put your pocket change toward a more substantial effort. Better yet, consider volunteering to work with one of these groups. Most of them need volunteers at one point or another during the year. You don't have to make a life of this, but even someone who could spare a few hours now and again would be a Godsend. Be wary out there, but don't be heartless...

Critics Of The Good Samaritan

If you're a Good Samaritan of any sort, you'll be criticized. It's not a matter of IF you'll be criticized for your Samaritanly efforts; it's a matter of WHEN you'll be criticized. This is one of the areas which often come up as a topic of conversation when I sit down and talk with other wary Samaritans. We're uniformly saddened by this and bewildered as to why it's so common. It's a truth in our society many people like to sit on the sidelines and complain about what others do, regardless of what it is. I've noticed social media seem to have exacerbated this as people feel free to criticize the work of total strangers. I see it on Facebook®, on YouTube®, and in all sorts of letters to the editors features related to Internet reporting.

What can you do to avoid this? I suppose you could quit. But my guess is if you quit you'd have a handful of people who would criticize that choice as well. They'd follow a vein similar to this, "She gave up just when all those poor people were counting on her to provide them with shoes for the winter." Now mind you, they never took any time previously to commend the lady with the shoe ministry, but they'll certainly find time to criticize her and its demise. The other thing you might try is to do all your good works in stealth mode. In stealth mode you do your best to always stay under the radar and never come up into anybody's conscious awareness. I know individuals and ministries which have operated like this for years and it works well for them.

The other form I see these attacks take is what Shakespeare might have termed, "...damning them with faint praise." This passive-aggressive form of criticism is popular and the folks who are expert at it come off looking like they really care about your pitiful, delusional, or terribly misguided efforts. These are the ones who comment on YouTube® and start off with something like, "I really enjoyed your 74 part series on learning how to be a machinist." Then they shift tactics with, "I was of course troubled that you chose to use the Sakamoto 1234 engine lathe, since it's not made in America and your touting it in these lessons will no doubt lead to the loss of manufacturing jobs here in the United States." First the poster appears to be saying thanks and suddenly pulls off the classic passive-aggressive ploy of decrying the choice of the means the wary Samaritan used as a teaching tool. And yes I do think teaching people how to perform a valuable skill is a very good work.

There are innumerable other examples I could offer here, but I suspect those of you who've fallen victim to these attacks could write your own book on them. My own experience is one

I share with you in that this happened to me so often in my 20s that I frequently was at the point of despair. I did the best I knew how with what I had, and still critics arose. My former pastor told me I would either have to learn to ignore the criticism and let it roll off of my back, or eventually I'd be drowned by it and give up altogether. In time, after years of continuously trying, I realized one day I was no longer even listening to my critics. Of course I still made mistakes and God knows I haven't been anywhere near perfect in the Good Samaritanly efforts I've made over the years since.

If you try long enough, you'll learn that if you don't become weary in your well-doing, you'll eventually see the benefits of your good works in God's time. Ignore the people who've made a life of being critics. For some of my own efforts it's taken decades between planting the seed and seeing the fruits of the harvest. Some of my critics I've won over... the rest eventually grew tired, found other people to criticize who'd pay them attention, or they grew old and died.

Spotting Hidden Need

We've all seen those pictures where objects are hidden in plain sight and we're asked to find them. The level of need in the world around us is similar to those pictures. We have a lot of needs around us which go unmet because not all need is obvious, as it's hidden in plain sight. If you come upon a man lying on a roadside unconscious and you see signs he's been attacked and wounded, most of us would understand immediately there was a need for action. The trickiest part of this whole wary situation doesn't come about from those times need is blatantly obvious. It comes about when need is blatantly obvious and the needy have been taught not to admit they have a need. In some instances they will not do so even if this means they and/or their children go hungry or sick.

I had a neighbor years back whose confused mess of a husband just up one day and left her to fend for 3 little kids. He'd never been one to bother much with steady work and the responsibility of a wife and kids apparently no longer appealed to him. The wife had a 32 hour a week job as a teacher's aide, which paid her less than $10 dollars an hour. I could see the signs in a matter of months as the gas was shut off, people came looking for the husband for money he owed them, and both she and the children showed the strain of their predicament in their faces. The mother would accept offers of produce from my garden and the garden of her other immediate neighbor, but wouldn't take money which he and I both offered. I gave her a list of agencies which could help; she refused to call them. She said her parents had warned her about the husband and they had raised her to pay her own way. She also admitted she and her husband had come to California to get away from her family because they despised her husband for frequently neglecting his wife and kids.

This went from bad to worse over a period of 6 months. I resorted to hiring the oldest child, a teenager, to rake the lawn or other small tasks as a pretense in order to give them money through the work. The day she and the kids were evicted from the home they'd been buying, I overheard the two youngest children, ages 5 and 7, talking about being hungry. Their mother was clearly exhausted as she hauled off load after load of their belongings to storage in their aging mini-van. When dark came they were loading up the last of their belongings and the little ones asked about food each time their mom came out the door with an arm load. She'd refused to look my way all day and had apparently told the children to do the same. I finally and insistently called her to the fence which separated our homes and held out a $100 dollar bill. At first she refused as always, but she relented when I said, "We often pray for God's help and when it finally comes we don't recognize it." They soon drove away and I never heard from her again.

You see some people suffer quietly while all the squeaky needs garner the attention. If you've lived very long, by now you've seen the professionally needy. By this I mean they've become experts at letting everybody they meet know about their needs, pressuring others to meet their needs, and not showing the least indication of embarrassment. You might want to take a more considered approach to ferreting out need as you move on in life and move past the squeaky crowd. Is that child hungry? Is that elderly neighbor ill or need medication? Does that family home appear to have had the utilities cut off? There are tragedies taking place around us regularly and to the people they're happening to they're never minor and every bit as threatening to life and limb as if they'd been set upon by thieves and were lying unconscious by the roadside.

Moving Toward The Danger

Recent terrible terrorist events in Massachusetts and the explosion in Texas underscore something about Good Samaritans of all sorts. You're no doubt aware of the bombs which went off at the Boston Marathon and of the fertilizer plant which exploded in the city of West, Texas. In each of those two very different cases, both life and death situations, while some people fled in terror, which is a perfectly natural reaction, others moved toward the danger to try and help. I contend those who raced to the bomb blast victims in Boston were every bit as brave as those who went into the flames in West, Texas and did not come out alive.

In both of the above instances when faced with a potentially lethal unknown these brave men and women ignored a clear danger to themselves, choked down the human inclination toward self-preservation, and raced to help those who were injured and dying. They ignored their own welfare to consider the welfare of others. As I ponder these events I'm reminded of a passage in John's Gospel and I'll paraphrase it here. "There is no greater love than when one man is willing to lay down his life for another man." Wary Samaritans everywhere have been hearing and heeding this message in one form or another for centuries... and they still keep moving toward the danger.

Sometimes Five Minutes Is Enough

I was the first upon the scene of the immediate aftermath of a hit and run last Thursday at a traffic light which borders a nearby city. The late model sedan was halfway out in the lane and the radiator and hood were sheared off. An elderly man sat behind the wheel with an air bag deployed, clearly stunned. The other car had just as clearly fled the scene and left the old man to his own devices. It took me a second to realize what had occurred, since there was only the one car and no one else around this country-city intersection. I pulled over and once I was sure the old man wasn't in immediate danger I called 911 and explained the situation. Shortly, the dispatcher came back on the line and told me the California Highway Patrol and an ambulance were on their ways.

By this time several other drivers and a lady from a nearby house had joined the scene and were talking with the old man in an effort to try and determine the extent of his injuries. Sensing he was in good hands and there didn't appear to be any danger of leaking fuel or a fire, I slipped back out of the now burgeoning crowd and got back into my truck and made my way on to my office. As I rolled away it occurred to me all of this had taken less than five minutes of my appointment-filled day. You see, a wary Samaritan isn't oblivious to the time constraints of his or her life. In fact, most wary Samaritans seem to be very conscious of their limitations in terms of what they can do or give. However, a wary Samaritan doesn't let those things determine whether or not he or she will get involved.

Small Acts Of Kindness

More often than not it's the small acts of Good Samaritanism which are left to us! By this I mean in the day-to-day of our lives there aren't always life or death crises in front of us. It's been surprising to me over a lifetime how many of the acts of kindness I've done or witnessed, which I hear people comment about years later, were actually events or actions which seemed almost trivial to me at the time they occurred. Never underestimate your ability to make the world a better place by performing some small act of kindness. What may seem a small act to you or I, could be a matter of enormous importance to a person or persons in need.

Start At Home

It's been said "Charity begins at home." With this idea firmly in mind let's always be certain we aren't ignoring the need for a wary Samaritan in our home while we're out saving the world. I spent two decades in professional ministry. I know exactly how easy it is to overlook the needs of your own family and yourself while reaching out to a world which is constantly in need. I believe most professional helpers would agree with me when I say it does little good in the long run to reach out to others, if in the end you're in need of more help than you ever gave away.

CHAPTER 4

The Locusts Or The Satellite

A current plague of Locusts in Egypt and Israel reminded me of a heated discussion I was engaged in decades ago regarding the recurrence of plagues of Locust in Sub-Saharan Africa. I was an undergrad and in a semester length environmental science class when we were made aware of a then current argument going on in the charity and academic worlds regarding taking millions of dollars and either using it one time to eradicate a swarm of Locust which had moved into Sub-Saharan Africa or, to use the same amount of money to pay for a dedicated weather satellite to monitor rainfall in sub-Saharan Africa for many years to come. Now you're probably fully confused.

My classmates and I, like most of you who read this were scratching our heads trying to understand why two so seemingly disparate schools of thought had sprung up over the use of this money. Our professor went on to explain the life cycle of Locust is tied to the amount of rainfall which comes down in Northern Africa, just above the Sahara. In years where the rainfall exceeds a specific minimum amount (which currently slips my memory), the Locust are programmed to hatch, feed, and breed. Digressing for just a moment, many desert plants and animals have breeding and life cycles similarly tied to specific minimum amounts of rainfall. Consequently, knowing how much it rains can be a valuable tool to timing spraying while the Locust are still in their infancy, most vulnerable, and easiest to eradicate.

Based on these facts, and always the contrarian, I argued in favor of spending the money for the satellite, even if it meant this plague of Locust would descend upon the fields and orchards of the North at least one more time. My argument was no more persuasive with my classmates than were the arguments of scientists who pleaded with the United Nations for the money for the satellite instead of the pesticide. The end result was the money was spent to spray pesticides and was partially successful in slowing, but not stopping the hoard of locust. Hold in mind pesticides would be used either way. However, using them early in the life cycle each time would mean using less and almost a complete eradication of the Locusts while they were young and still the nesting sites.

There are times when each of us is faced with a problem similar to the locusts or the satellite dilemma. We see before us on our television or computer screens tragic images (e.g., famine, floods, earthquakes, tsunamis, storms, etc.), and our natural response is to react to the problem before us immediately (i.e., send your check today). A wary Samaritan learns over a lifetime when wise men have said things like, "The poor you have with you always," or "Sufficient to the day is the evil thereof," they weren't kidding. There's always some health epidemic waiting in the wings. There's always some natural disaster headed this way. There's always one more place where there are hungry children, sick, naked and without food. Knee-jerk reactions are viscerally satisfying; unfortunately they're not necessarily the most effective.

Are You Planting A Garden

Some years I plant bits and pieces of a garden. Some years I have no garden at all. This year is a year I'm making a bigger effort and I'm planting tomatoes, bitter melon, and some summer squash. I've also trellised some long-handled drinking gourds which my family has cultivated off and on for more than 70 years. Sometimes I skip a few years on the gourds, but eventually I replant to keep the tradition alive. My late brother Billy Joe passed those seeds along to me and I've done my best in the ensuing years to keep the line alive.

I want you to think for a minute of your garden as a Good Samaritan effort. I want you to do this because we live in a time when people have become so disconnected from what it actually takes to make a life that your garden is a 'magical' place to children and adults who've never had one. I have young adults and young children on both sides of my small 6,000 square foot yard. This proximity offers the perfect teaching opportunity; I greedily latch onto it.

I share gardening tips with them. I talk to them about the health benefits of fresh produce. I point up to them it's the cheapest way to get the freshest and most nutritious veggies at any time of the year. I talk to them about how healthy and family oriented and activity gardening is. I'm unabashedly pro-gardening. Have you ever considered how something as simple as sharing your gardening know-how can be a major-league Good Samaritan effort?

Avoiding The Spotlight

As surprising as it may seem, there are people who will actively try to wreck the works of a wary Samaritan. I'm seeing this right now in a group I work with. There's a former member of the group who won't participate because he felt he didn't get the accolades he deserved. He further complained to other members he felt he should be honored and hadn't been. He's campaigned regularly ever since to promote himself and his choices by denigrating others who've been honored. Since I'm not in charge of accolades, the only insight I can venture is the people who've been honored to this point are all years older than this fellow, and for that matter, years older than his nominees. The recipients each have a body of good works spanning several decades and are either fully or semi-retired.

Many wary Samaritans spend their lives trying to remain out of the spotlight while other people seem to spend their lives trying to get into the spotlight. I'm sure if we psychoanalyzed these situations we'd be able to see what drives both groups. But this seems a fool's errand and I'm not saying one approach is any better than the other. I will venture the observation getting into the spotlight and staying in the spotlight are two entirely different matters and require two different skill sets. The original Good Samaritan seems to have been from the avoiding the spotlight crowd. We don't even have his name or the whole area of good works would be named after him personally instead of a genericized tag related to his religious or ethnic group.

Regardless of tags, there's little doubt we live in an age of self-promotion. Some of this comes from it being a competitive world and the accompanying need to be recognized in order to thrive in one's career. Some of it seems to stem from certain people's need to receive adulation all the time. Others have posited it's a birth order issue or some similar blow to the psyche which drives this phenomenon. However, in the area of Good Samaritanism it seems to go entirely against the grain to try and garner the spotlight in a calling which prides itself on anonymity. I support the concept of people being honored for the body of their life's work. But the pursuit of recognition and the spirit of competitiveness which accompanies it seem to be entirely out of place amongst wary Samaritans.

Pencils Or Bullets

I was listening yesterday to a recent research poll, which was conducted in predominantly Muslim countries, regarding attitudes toward some of the harsher aspects of Islam (e.g., suicide bombers, honor killings, killing infidels, etc.). The numbers were particularly disturbing, with as many as 28% of Muslims interviewed worldwide favoring these abhorrent practices. With an estimated 1,600,000,000 Muslims residing on planet Earth, the poll would imply there are as many as 448,000,000 Muslims out there who favor religious practices detestable to most people of faith, regardless of the faith being practiced.

About the same time I was also thinking about how ineffective wars have been at getting the Muslim people to embrace a less violent approach to faith and in how one goes about making converts to one's religion. I recalled a young man from my hometown, who while serving in the United States military in Afghanistan convinced people back home to donate tons of classroom materials to be used in education of both Muslim boys and Muslim girls. This was and is controversial among the harshest Muslim sects and one of the efforts groups like the Taliban and more recently ISIS decry. By their interpretation it violates Sharia law.

I have to wonder if in the long run the Taliban, ISIS, and other similarly situated Muslim groups have more to fear from educated men and women from their own countries than they do from the weapons of the British, the French, the Russians, and the Americans. It's entirely possible what little education was assimilated by the masses before such education was cut off, will be more destructive to these doctrines of hate in the long-run than all the munitions expended. The pencils given away by one wary Samaritan may be far more powerful than bullets in changing hearts and lives.

I Can't Go There Anymore

A friend of mine and I were discussing places in the world where we'd like to be able to help and he mentioned his wife was considering going to a certain country as a short-term volunteer. He was surprised when I told him I no longer give time or money to try and fix this particular nation. His surprise stemmed from the fact he'd known me for two decades and had previously seen me make two major efforts to raise funds for those same people. He chuckled, knowing my reputation as an increasingly wary Samaritan and wondered out loud what had soured me on this continuously bedeviled country.

I share with you now, what I shared with him then. At 61 years of age and rapidly approaching 62, I'm increasingly aware of the finiteness of my own existence and the physical and financial limitations on what I can do and how many more years I can do it. I look at rotten monarchies, dysfunctional dictatorships, and all out no-mans-lands differently than I did as I was approaching age 32. I find myself looking for what basketball players call the high percentage shot. If I give money, or more precious yet the days of my life, I want it to be used effectively. I don't want to throw any more Hail Marys with more heart than head.

I'm no longer supporting places which have been the source of dozens of humanitarian crises in my lifetime because I've seen blood, sweat, tears, and billions poured into these humanitarian bottomless pits again and again. Routinely their crises boondoggles are later exposed as the work of political grifters; clever thieves grow rich on the well-intentioned donations of the gullible. I don't even have to mention their names; you know the countries as well as I do. I'm no longer supporting NGOs, ministries, or non-profits who beg me through every form of media to lend a helping hand just one more time in these money pits. I don't have to call them by name; you know the names of the NGOs, ministries, and non-profits just as well as I do.

In more than 40 years along this wary Samaritan highway, I've grown warier and I've grown wiser. My heart is not hardened to the tremendous need throughout the world. However, my heart has become hardened to the victims I kept finding in the same ditch, attacked by the same villains, in the same manner for the 4th or 5th or 6th time. I've discovered there are victims who have yet to meet a single Good Samaritan for the 1st time. I find it rather refreshing to see victims become victims no more. You younger and more optimistic Good Samaritans can have your turn on the repeat victim nations with my blessing.

One of the fundamental lessons of my young life was from my protestant mother. She often said to her children, "The Lord helps those who help themselves." This was aimed at me and my siblings in order to remind us there was a certain amount of effort God was looking for us to put forth before we fell on our faces and cried for a miraculous rescue. I see a mantle of victimhood which many people today have embraced, both domestically and internationally. I've come to believe the people of some countries may be forced to face absolute life and death (not just the more-favored constantly near-death status) before they'll rise up against their oppressors, lift a hand to save themselves, and either die or move forward as a free people.

Until perpetual victims reach the point where they're desperate enough they'll throw themselves against their despoilers and corrupt political systems, which have kept them and their ancestors as virtual slaves for decades, all the well-intentioned efforts and mountains of cash sent by you and me will ever do is ameliorate their problems just enough so they can move back to the near-death status. Wary Samaritans, I think it's time to step away and aid others who have yet to receive such aid for the 1st time. Meanwhile, the chronic victims might finally get fed up with being victimized and revolt instead of being appeased with a visit from Hollywood, the World Bankers, and the promises of the United Nations.

Who Gains And Who Loses?

I'm writing this in response to a question I received by email regarding some writings posted on my TheWarySamaritan blog. I asked there why would a despot and his or her henchmen be ecstatic to see Christian ministries, non-profits, and NGOs roll in when their nation's systems fail for the umpteenth time? Why would our greatest humanitarian leaders be coerced into being pictured in countless photos taken with these vilest of human beings? Why's there suddenly a relaxing of heretofore strict religious laws in the land while these aid workers and their money is in the country?

Here's why! Those parasitic leaders around the world feed upon the poorest of the poor, live in opulent palaces, cavort with the Jet Set, and eat and drink every day like ancient potentates. Meanwhile they routinely steal the best their countries have to offer and what they don't directly consume they hide in covert bank accounts and dubious overseas investments. They're therefore only too happy to see the do-gooders show up with humanitarian aid in the form of a fresh supply of food, medicine, shelter, clothes, or cash.

This help keeps the populace from rioting and any chance of a potential overthrow of the true source of the nation's troubles.

It also ensures at every level of the local bureaucracy, from the lowliest neighborhood apparatchik to the head Mogul himself, bureaucrats both great and small will be able to settle in for another feed on the blood of the dying. This cycle needs to be broken. This cycle does not deserve to be fed again. Be observant of the peoples and the world around you and don't just tear open your wallet the next time you hear there's a need in some despot's vision of Utopia.

Good Deed Multiplication

I especially like to be able to donate to causes I believe in where there are corporate donors who'll match my donation. It's become a popular approach with many corporate citizens as they try to remain relevant to the day-to-day existence of mankind. As a wary Samaritan you should check with your favorite worthy causes to see if they have donors who are willing to work these kinds of matches. It's also a good idea to speak with your employer to see if they may do any kind of matching of employee charitable contributions. These days there's enormous competition for donor dollars. If you truly believe in and support a cause, go the extra mile to find ways to extend what you donate.

Are You Wary Enough

I catch a lot of flak from my adult children because I'm always after them to have a minimum of a three-week supply of food and water on hand in their homes in the event of an emergency. It used to only be a one-week supply but times have changed. As a wary Samaritan, I'm always concerned about what can go wrong in our world which would put every Good Samaritan to the test.

I want to list some events every family, whether they live in the city or the country, should be prepared to encounter and survive without any outside help, for a period of at least three weeks. These appear in no particular order, but take in all areas of the nation. I want to close by saying unless you can in good conscience kill your hungry neighbors or watch them starve or die of thirst; you might want to lay in a few extra items.

1. Ice Storm
2. Hurricane
3. Blizzard
4. Tornado
5. Tsunami
6. Earthquake
7. Nuclear Reactor Malfunction
8. Terrorist Attack
9. Flood
10. Labor Strike closing off transportation or international shipping ports
11. Drought
12. Solar Flare Induced Electromagnetic Pulse (EMP)
13. Nuclear Weapon Induced Electromagnetic Pulse (EMP)
14. Celestial Object Impact Event (i.e., meteorite, comet, space debris, etc.)
15. Pandemic (e.g., plague, flu, virus, etc.)
16. Wildfires and Firestorm Events
17. Volcanic Eruption
18. Nuclear Detonation 10,000 Miles Away (Indirect Effects)
19. Nuclear Detonation at the Nearest Military Base (Direct Effects)
20. Nuclear Detonation on a major city (Direct attack)
21. Dust Storm
22. Economic Collapse

I Can't Treat Dead

I had the opportunity recently to help a neighbor lady who'd suffered a serious health event. Her blood sugar had fallen dangerously low and after nearly crashing her car in an effort to get it stopped, she'd slumped over the steering wheel in her driveway. I heard the commotion, but just figured she'd screeched to a halt accidentally and paid it no attention until one of her children began to call my name. When I ran outside in response to the urgency in the child's voice, he said, "Can you help my mother, she's sick and can't get out of the car." I immediately rushed to the car and began to assess the situation and ask her questions.

Even with my limited hands-on health care experience, I could tell she was either suffering heart attack, having a *Petite Mal* seizure, or the victim of low potassium or blood sugar. We laid her back in the car seat, mopped her face with a cool cloth, and reassured her she was going to be okay. I simultaneously instructed her husband to call 911 and get some professional help on the way. The ambulance and Fire Department arrived within five minutes and transported her to the local hospital. After a couple of I.V. bags of sugar-water her blood sugar rose from 64 to nearly 120 and she came home to her husband and three little kids.

A couple of points here I feel bear mentioning. Despite having gone to law school and heard all those horror stories in Tort lectures about assuming liability and creating a special legal relationship where none existed before, I knew California has a Good Samaritans' law which allows me to assist the sick or injured so long as I don't try to play physician. Of course you have to know the extent of your abilities and not exceed them. As a wary Samaritan, if your state doesn't have some similar law you need to be working to see one put into place. On any given day, any of us could need the help of a Good Samaritan from similar circumstances to those I've described.

If help is delayed or denied for fear of lawsuits for getting involved, you or someone you love could advance from simply being ill or injured to being dead. I recall once being told over the phone by an emergency room physician to perform a process on my infant daughter, which I thought was questionable and it scared me. He'd instructed me to place her in a cold shower due to an extremely high fever. The ER physician must have heard the hesitation in my voice and said, "Sir, I can treat this illness once you get her here, but if you don't do as I instruct you right now and get this fever down, I can't treat brain damage and I can't treat dead."

It's okay to be a wary Samaritan, but don't be so wary you'd let your neighbor die!

In Hindsight

A phone call late this afternoon from a local newspaper reporter reminded me how one of my Good Samaritan actions almost 30 years ago did more to turn me into a wary Samaritan than all the others combined. After I'd agreed to meet with her later this week for an interview, I began once again to ponder the cost of Good Samaritanism. For some I've known, the cost was their life. So for me to still be here enjoying this life, my wife, my children, and my grandchildren while others have died to follow this path, I can't in good conscience complain or say I would do anything different than what I've previously done. This path is not always easy... but it's always right!

If You Give Your Body To Be Burned
I like to remind other wary Samaritans we can only give to others those things which we already possess. It's important to remember we shouldn't become so overburdened in reaching out to those we find in the ditch we neglect our own health, our own relationships, our own welfare, or the welfare of our families. Case in point, I ran into an old high school classmate a few days ago who's he's devoted his life to ministry in general and church planting in particular. As we chatted and he shared his health challenges, he admitted many of them were stress related. He'd recently become so ill he had to take a sabbatical just to get medical attention for a couple of these problems. I feel fairly confident the whole mindset surrounding Good Samaritanism wasn't and shouldn't be we destroy ourselves in trying to make other people whole. The older I get the more this self-destructive approach seems antithetical to Good Samaritanism.

It's A Good Thing
Having passed age 61 I find I have more and more personal items (e.g., books, tools, and memorabilia) I've acquired in life which I no longer need or use. I've begun the process of shedding some of these items by finding younger men and women who could actually make use of my old treasures. In this way I can lighten the load from my own home, gain space, help my kids not have to work through all my belongings when my passing finally comes, and I can make someone else's life better right now. Even a wary Samaritan knows when you can accomplish a win-win-win, it's a good thing.

Kick It Up A Notch
Many a wary Samaritan tries to pass along to their children and grandchildren the values which go along with tangibly helping

others and reaching out to those in distress. I find modeling good behavior goes much further than just talking about good behavior. Most of the major religions admonish their adherents to be active in living out their faith. Talking about good works, hearing about good works, and suggesting good works to others can all be positive things. However, actually getting your hands into the dirty work of Good Samaritanism takes the expression of your faith, and you, to an entirely different level.

Finding An Alternative Good Work

Last Thursday morning I heard my neighbor cranking his vehicle again and again. It didn't sound good and I could tell he was running the battery down to no effect. Like many folks my age, he and his wife are helping to raise their grandkids and part of that task involves getting them down to the middle school daily. When I went outside to put some papers into my vehicle to take to the office, his Grandson asked me if I had a set of jumper cables and could jump his Grandfather's vehicle. I knew I didn't have any with me and shared this sad bit of news with him so he could take it to his Grandfather. A few minutes later I heard him make a final attempt at a start, and the battery was completely drained.

I stepped back outside, called out to the Grandson, and asked him which middle school he attended. He told me the name and told me his younger sister went there as well. "Why don't you ask your Grandfather if it would be okay if I drive you and your sister to school?" He was off in a flash and in less than a minute came hurrying back with his book bag, backpack and the younger sister, who was similarly burdened down. I told them we'd take my wife's Camry, since it's a four door and easier to get into than my Silverado. The ride to school took less than five minutes. In another five minutes I was back at my house and preparing to go about my day. My neighbor called out his thanks to me as I headed in to finish getting ready for work.

As a wary Samaritan, I can't always do exactly what I'm asked to do and neither can you. When this happens I often look to see if there is a useful alternative which might resolve the dilemma. In this instance the real problem was getting the youngsters to school on time. Once this was accomplished Grandfather had almost eight hours to figure out what was wrong with his pickup. Sometimes we can't help at all, sometimes we can help exactly in the manner we're asked to, and sometimes we have to search for alternative good works which meet the core need. When I got home that afternoon the kids were playing in their yard, the Grandfather was gone to the garage with his truck, and the Grandmother rocked a baby still too young for school. It all worked out okay; even if it didn't work out the way it might have if jumper cables had been on hand.

Beggars Versus The Needy

I apologize in advance as this is a recurring theme in my writing, but it presents itself in all its iterations before me almost daily, so it's hard to ignore. Now that the weather is warming up in our area as spring comes on in full force, I notice the busy street corners have begun to fill up again with all the hungry and homeless sign bearers who seemed to have disappeared over the winter. For whatever reason you can imagine, they seem to be the same hungry and homeless people who've worked those street corners for the past four or five years. I'm unsure if they hibernate or if they move along to the snowbird climes of Arizona, but in either case the do return with the good weather.

I find it both clever and revealing they work the busy intersections off the Interstate where most of their benefactors/victims are out of the area travelers who haven't previously seen them in their steady business of homelessness. Now if you knew this wary Samaritan well, you'd know I do care about the truly hungry and truly homeless, but I'm infuriated by people who use these monikers as a way to scam the general public for money, drugs, alcohol, or just to live out a life without any meaningful contribution to society. I will say again here what I routinely say in speaking and writing, *Caveat Emptor* as you go about doing good works.

Good Samaritans Outnumber Thieves

For all its faults, The United States is a truly amazing nation and its citizens a very generous people. As I write this passage I've been looking at the devastation shown on the nightly news of the destruction wreaked upon Moore, Oklahoma by a massive Tornado. As much as I cringe at the pictures of the devastation, I'm always heartened to see people pull together and come to one another's aid in times of crises. The people of Moore and the surrounding communities have been joined by people from across the Midwest to repair the damage done and help restore all those disrupted lives.

Everywhere I looked there were in the video footage there were examples of people helping now and in some cases having nearly died during to save others. This is Good Samaritanism at its very best. This is the kind of coming together communities need to experience regularly and not just in times of crises. Now having said all that I've no doubt there'll be sporadic reports of looting because there are always those kinds of despicable people among us. I have an equal degree of certainty we'll hear of and see far more of Good Samaritans at work than thieves there among this Tornado's destructive path. Today the good people of Moore, Oklahoma (and their neighbors) steeped off the busy road and onto the calamitous roadside to assist their fellow man.

He Wasn't The Perfect Samaritan

I go back periodically to look at my Scofield edition of the original King James version of The Holy Bible with regard to the story of the Good Samaritan. This edition was one I used as a pulpit Bible for all my years of ministry and I especially liked it because the sections of scripture are carved up by topic with a nice large print header across the column. In this case it uses the term "Good Samaritan" to highlight for the reader the information to follow. In preaching God's word and in lawyering man's law, individual words have enormous impact on everything else with which they appear. The same can be said of this seminal passage for all who would be Good Samaritans.

Now I hope this teaser has you wondering just a little bit about what it is I'm driving at. It is in fact the use of the word "Good" as a description instead of the use of words like poor, adequate, or perfect. I am especially drawn to the fact that the word good doesn't appear here in the King James text; I'm extremely grateful the word perfect doesn't either. I've never been a perfect Samaritan. I cannot recall having ever met a perfect Samaritan or even the better Samaritan. There are times I've been a poor Samaritan, but much of the time I'm merely an adequate or Good Samaritan. Good seems proper because perfect applied to my own efforts, and likely yours, would be hyperbole.

When Jesus shared this story it was with a man identified as an expert in the Jewish law. The man had asked him about how to inherit eternal life. Later in trying to defend himself the same man asked Jesus who his neighbor was. It's then Jesus tells the story we're all familiar with. If you're unaware of the facts, the Jews and the Samaritans had an old animosity for one another based on a religious disagreement. For Jesus to offer a source of religious animosity as an example of fulfilling the law to a man identified as an expert in the law, was likely an affront. To hold a Samaritan up as an example to be followed if one wished to inherit eternal life had to be galling at the very least.

Now to get more firmly back on my original point, if you or I in our efforts to live out the Good Samaritan credo are offered to people as exemplars, expect some push back; perfect Samaritans we are not. In this writing I offer examples of other people's lives (and my own life) who are trying to be Good Samaritans despite their misgivings, fears, and failures. Thinking back to grade school I recalled the terms good, better, and best and how they were often applied to progressively denote improved quality. Jesus never offers another story about a better Samaritan or a best Samaritan. I think this is because none of us could have measured up too better or best, much less perfect.

In the best light of the Gospel, each of us can never be better than "sinners saved by grace." I know this grates against any hint of narcissism or the sense we can save ourselves, but there you have it. We're sinful by birth and that sin nature carries with it imperfection. We're imperfect in our minds, our bodies, our relationships, and even in how we relate to our Creator. I remind people all the time they need to lighten up on themselves. Don't take yourself too seriously in life; very few others do. In trying to be a Good Samaritan you'll make mistakes and you'll be an embarrassment to yourself at times. However, you'll never have to worry about being perfect.

CHAPTER 5

Give Gifts With Lasting Meaning

Back when the 2014 Holiday Season was approaching, my wife Huong and I were able to help some children in third world receive Polio vaccinations. UNICEF had a wonderful program for giving immunizations in lieu of regular gifts at that time of year. She and I now donate to the UNICEF vaccine program regularly and will be joining them again this year in their efforts in Polio eradication.

Many wary Samaritans are old enough to have had childhood acquaintances that suffered with polio. They also have images in their minds of iron lungs and leg braces. They'll also easily remember the Manhattan Project-like approach taken in their own communities aimed at stamping out Polio in the United States. I know these images are a permanent part of my own memories of childhood.

Children here initially endured shots and then later received sugar cubes with the vaccine absorbed into the cube. Normally, I can't stand the United Nations and won't get into their politics here. But I've been pleasantly surprised now for more than a decade with UNICEF and its health vaccination programs. I know there are other fine organizations out there that've joined the vaccination battle and I salute them too.

If you're not already a donor, consider UNICEF's effort and please check them out at http://www.UNICEF.org

Learning And Teaching New Tricks

Over the years it's become apparent to me not only have the times changed, the needs have changed as well. I used to take staples (e.g., beans, rice, oats, milk, corn meal, flour, sugar, vegetable oil, and assorted vegetables, etc.), to the local food bank, Catholic Charities, or other similar feeding programs. I also used to give those kinds of things to families who were in need of food. In many cases this won't work anymore. What I'm asked for by these feeding programs today is boxed cereal, foods which can be eaten without warming, foods which can be warmed in an oven or microwave, and food items such as canned spaghetti or raviolis. These don't sound particularly nutritious to me but being a nutrition expert isn't my purpose here either.

At first I was puzzled by this request and even a little bit annoyed at what has become of our nation. But as I observed younger families shopping at the local market it became evident many young men and women are no longer able to produce a wholesome meal for themselves or their children from basic food staples. Microwave items and food items which can be warmed and served are the basis (for bad or for good) of the diet of many modern households. An added consideration is that of parents who are unable to prepare meals due to their use of drugs, alcohol, or suffering from mental illness; this leaves the little ones to their own limited preparation abilities. I think programs to teach the bulk of these families how to use basic foods and prepare a healthy meal are sorely needed. Apparently, even our government agencies which used to do this kind of life skills training have all but abandoned their efforts.

You see, the meal hungry people are most worried about right now is their next one; nutritional value or the lack thereof is a distant secondary consideration. If I as a wary Samaritan were in a country experiencing a famine, I'd be trying to keep them alive; we're in a famine of sorts here in this country. I'm all for teaching survival skills to the younger generations. But in the meantime, in all good conscience you and I can't just stand by angry at their lack of domestic skills and allow them go hungry, especially the children. A two-pronged need lies before us. First, we need to reach out as best we can to the immediate food needs which face us, and second we need to find or develop teaching programs at our houses of faith and other community groups to offer basic life skills which the state no longer sees as necessary.

It's Still The Small Details

I'm told manners were developed to help maintain a civil society and to keep us from constantly taking offense and injuring one another. If you've studied any psychology in this area you've ran across the works of Konrad Lorenz' on *aggression inhibiting behaviors* and *aggression inhibiting responses*, there he explores the small acts of civility which aid our violent species in survival and maintaining a civil society.

This made me think about how often we erroneously believe it's the big things we do as good deeds which matter most in the larger scheme of things. Truth be told, I find it's the small and seemingly insignificant acts of assistance or kindness which provide the oil which lubricates what otherwise might be a very rough gearbox of human contact.

So, when you feel like the little things you do to make the world a better place don't matter much, stop and think again! Every wary Samaritan has those questioning days where we wonder if we truly make a difference or if we're just deluding ourselves. To this path of introspection I'd like to reassure each of you, you make more of a difference than you'll ever know in this life.

Be Wary Of The Pretenders

This wary Samaritan was in the parking lot of a large shopping center about 200 yards from a major freeway interchange. I'd just come from one of the business establishments in this overgrown strip mall and made it out to my car on the far North edge of the lot. You see, one of the concessions I've made to aging is to park further and further from the place I wish to shop in order to force myself to walk those extra steps each day. When I arrived back at my truck I saw another man about my age pull up in a late model van at about the same time. As I was preparing to leave I paused for a moment to see if he too was going to walk all the extra distance to the strip of businesses 400 feet south of us. Instead, he rummaged around in the side door of his van and came out with a dirty old bandanna, a tattered piece of cardboard, and a cane. I was puzzled by this and wondered what on earth this had to do with coming to a strip mall.

A moment later, after putting on the bandanna and tucking the cardboard under his arm, he took the cane into his right hand and was immediately transformed into a 'pitiful cripple' reminiscent of a full-blown Dicken's character. I use this term specifically because his stature and gait were instantly morphed to the stature and gait of a man with a severe physical handicap. Handicaps I might add which were not evident all the while he was locating his props. He looked around the parking lot and froze as he caught me staring at him. His gaze never shifted and his countenance remained as one who's born all life's heavier burdens. Seeing I was the only one who had witnessed this transformation, he slowly turned toward the freeway interchange and hobbled away, cardboard tucked neatly beneath his arm. I was another few minutes putting my purchases away and readying to leave, then three more minutes at the light. When I got to the on-ramp, there he stood; the sign said 'Disabled Veteran' and 'God Bless'; the car ahead of me had come to a stop to give him a bill.

I've Been Taken Again

If you're anything like I am, you've reached out to those in need by lending tools, equipment, repair manuals, cookbooks, or other tangible objects. You did this because you saw their need and wanted to help meet it. The net result is your conscience is clear in the matter because you know you've done the best you could do. This is generally a great feeling and the endorphins it releases reinforces future similar behavior. Now moving forward the item you've loaned gets returned 95% of the time in as good of a condition as it left you. These events always make you happy and affirm your faith in your fellow man.

But if you're a true wary Samaritan you know once in a while the item you lent will come back broken, torn, greasy, or unusable. It's also the same 5% of the recipients who never mention the damage or offer to make things whole. You can do one of two things, you can cuss and scream and cry about the injustice which has been done to you and your possessions, OR you can accept this is part of the price paid by each Good Samaritan throughout the course of their lives. I'm not saying you need to be a doormat for abusive types. What I'm saying is we must count the loss as part of the price we pay to be able to help the other 95%.

Placing Your Life At Risk

I was thinking yesterday about my father's penchant for bringing home strangers as guests for breakfast, lunch, dinner, or the week. From my earliest memories there were strangers at our table who might only be there once, never to be seen again, or they might appear several days in a row and never to be seen again. This was one of his ways of helping people who were down and out. He'd help them find work, feed them, and at times even give them a place to spend the night. These strangers turned out to be fascinating to me as a young boy and at other times they were scary. I believe the 1950s and 1960s were a less crazy time than today and in general it might've been safe to be this open. But on at least one occasion we later learned we'd fed and housed three people wanted by law enforcement for serious felonies.

Be cautious out there. Whether you're male or female, you have to take a moment to assess any potential Good Samaritan action for all the pros and cons immediately present. As a wary Samaritan, I want you to be wary. Is the man or woman in the ditch really injured, or is it a ruse to get you to stop so he or she and his cohorts might assault and rob you? I've pointed out in my speaking and writing on this topic over the years how I've been taken advantage of at times. Only once do I ever recall the perpetrators getting near my family and in that instance it was a young couple with an infant son. They eventually managed to burglarize the parsonage we lived in before they left town. This betrayal was how they repaid a week of food, shelter, and medical attention for their infant son. I've never let anyone get so close to my house or my family again. I'm not bitter, I'm wary.

Here's my point! I don't think God expects you to risk your life or the lives of your spouse or children just to perform a Good Deed. I know this may go against everything you've heard in your lifetime, but it's my view. Now understand I do think you can engage in otherwise risky acts of helping safely, if you first take the time to engage appropriate safeguards. But the idea of dashing headlong into every problem we encounter now seems foolhardy to me at best. I caution you about putting your life or the lives of your loved ones at risk. This is not 1956 and we're all aware of the proliferation of evil in the world around us. So on your journey as a wary Samaritan, don't become an accident or crime statistic. We already have plenty of examples in those areas; we don't need to add your tragic tale to those already out there.

Well Done

I suspect when all of life is over and people stand before the Creator, there'll truly be those who arrive full of themselves. They'll of course depart deflated when their self-important efforts are judged paltry or useless. I also suspect there'll be those who arrive with much trepidation and concern about the meager offerings of time, money, and talent which life allowed them to make, only to discover the Creator has seen both what they had and what they did with it and hear him respond, "Well done thou good and faithful servant."

People Just Needing A Break
We've had graduations going on in our community all of this past week and they'll continue next week too. Each day different junior high schools and high schools were graduating their current crop of students. I believe the local colleges and the universities all held their ceremonies last month as well, so the rest of the month appears to be clear on the graduation ceremony front. I shared all those details with you in order to say this, I saw several people at the market last week allowing other people who were clearly loaded down with graduation trappings (e.g., cards, flowers, cakes, balloons, cupcakes, etc.) to go ahead of them in the checkout line. I did it myself for an anxious looking young man with a large bouquet of flowers and a box of chocolates. He explained to me he was late to his younger sister's 8th grade graduation as he moved ahead of me in the queue. My point here is not all acts of kindness or compassion have to take place on the roadside; sometimes a wary Samaritan is needed in the checkout line at the local market as well.

Would You Do It For Jesus
I believe it was Jesus who said something to the effect of if we do something (good or bad) to the lowliest human being, it's as if we'd done it to him. Now I like the positive side of this equation when I've done something kind, thoughtful, or even life changing for someone. I like it a whole lot less when I've done something wrong to someone and the negative is on my side of the ledger.

It's funny how these things work both ways and it's clear from the context it isn't enough just to go out and do good works. It's annoying to me how we're expected to also be doing no harm to anyone or it's as if we've done it to Jesus. There's a lot more too this wary Samaritan business than meets the eye and it seems you have to look at both sides of the problem to be certain you're part of the solution and not part of the problem.

When I was a young man my Pastor, John Sciford, was fond of asking the congregation for a show of hands as to how many of us, "… love almost everybody." His point being there's room for improvement in even the best of us. We know this is true because we often (just as the scribe and the Pharisee did) cross to the other side of the road to avoid helping someone in need. I know you've got your reasons and I've got mine, but let's not pretend it never happens.

So the next time you're inclined to ignore the needs of one of those people in your life who always rubs you the wrong way, remember even the smallest acts of kindness (e.g., a cup of water, a piece of bread, basic shelter, clothes, etc.) appear to be something which God takes note of. Then remember throughout his life it was seemingly unimportant places to which Jesus was drawn, and seemingly unimportant people with whom he often sought interaction.

The values of a wary Samaritans are never the values of this world.

Sufficient To The Day Is The Evil Thereof

I'm unsure if I've mentioned it in these writing, but I was a Boy Scout after my Cub Scout days ended and the whole concept of doing a good deed daily is firmly ingrained in me from my earliest years to my teens. I like to remind myself (and you) that while it may be theoretically possible to perform a good deed every day, it's not always practically possible to do so. Chalk it up to other Good Samaritans busily about their own good deeds, fewer people falling into the path of thieves, or God simply giving you the day off. Enjoy the down time, tomorrow is a new day and generally there seems to be fewer wary Samaritans than there are situations in need of a wary Samaritan.

Knowledge Area Experts

Just about everyone I know is a *Knowledge Area Expert.* Some are endowed with this moniker by academic preparation, and some are known for their expertise based on a lifetime of valuable experiences. I value knowledge regardless of the means of the qualifications of its source. Most of us take our expertise for granted, as do our families and close friends. For instance, my mother took her homemade biscuits and chocolate gravy for granted and never taught me to make it (perhaps I should have paid closer attention when she was preparing it). Others have shared with me their expertise in how to operate machinery, craft a scientific experiment, or write a research paper. My life is richer for their sharing. I comment on this line of reasoning throughout my writings and encourage you wary Samaritans out there to never underestimate the value of sharing yourself with others.

Everyone I know seems to possess the power to change lives they come in contact with in some way or another; most times for the better, sometimes for the worse. Ironically, when I point this up to people they often dismiss their own abilities as being trivial. They're not trivial to those who need them. The first step in this process is to critically assess yourself and accept the places you're an expert; you'll also need to accept the places you're not. At this point you can confidently offer your assistance as a knowledge area expert in the places where it's appropriate and you can also be quiet in places where your silence is appropriate for. It's still far more preferable to this wary Samaritan to help people avoid falling among thieves and ending up on the roadside than to have to go into a roadside ditch to make the otherwise dramatic rescue. It's entirely possible the ditch could be avoided completely if we'd be willing to teach others what we already know.

Practical Good Samaritanism

In line with what I've been writing to you throughout this book about sharing yourself, I regularly share some similar thoughts on one of my blogs, *Almost A Wise Man* and in my second published work, *In Your Time: A Twentieth Century Grandfather Writes To His Twenty-first Century Grandchildren*. Recently I shared with my blog readers how to save themselves at least 60% of the cost of a new UPS (Uninterruptible Power Supply) by simply changing out the dead battery (i.e., this is the cause of UPS unit failures more than 80% of the time).

For a regular home computer user the savings as compared to buying a new UPS can easily be $65. For businesses such as mine, where we rely heavily on Servers, replacing the UPS battery packs can save as much a $1,200 over the cost of going down to the office supply and purchasing a new commercial unit. If you consider it for a moment, you'll think of other means of savings you know about which you could easily share. It requires no roadside heroics, no fighting of muggers, and no nursing someone back to health.

Now clearly this kind of wary Samaritanism isn't nearly as exciting as going to the rescue of someone who's been mugged, raped, or robbed. But for many people having an extra $65 - $1,200 in their pockets can mean the difference between groceries and no groceries or, if you're the boss the difference between paying yourself or not paying yourself this month. This goes back to what I've said here in other passages about how your practical efforts can tangibly change your life and the lives of others. Don't be dismissive of this approach or these kinds of efforts... they do make a difference.

Don't Get Fooled Again

A church a few blocks from my home is asking for donations for food for the homeless. I don't attend this particular church or belong to their denomination, but I know their history and their past good works. My wife and I will be contributing to this feeding project rather than sending money a thousand miles away to someone we've never met or heard of, who's asking for money to feed the homeless in a town we've never been to. My point here is you and I are responsible to be both good stewards and wary Samaritans. Make sure your good works aren't lining some con man's pockets. This doesn't mean there aren't good charities in other places, but local charities work locally and you can have a higher degree of oversight in order to be certain your giving isn't being abused.

A Tiny Vision

There is a danger in a charitable organization's efforts to deliberately minimize the size of their overall outreach. While I recognize there must be limits to the scope of a charitable effort for reasons of practicality, whenever I encounter organizations which have deliberately limited the scope of their work, despite a huge need and a correspondingly huge desire on the part of the giving public to help support their work, I'm dumbfounded.

I experienced this recently with a group who told me they didn't want to accept any more donations because they only had limited time for the project they'd started and hadn't expected it to be so successful. They didn't offer to direct me elsewhere. Even a wary Samaritan sees when an organization becomes the nexus between a societal ill and a means to correct such an ill, the organization's vision must be expanded to match the level of need or the resources will move on. These folks clearly didn't see it that way.

The projects I've worked with over the years, while clearly defining what they hope to accomplish with each effort, have also been willing to suggest alternative charities or ministries to send the donor too in the event they couldn't accommodate the donor. So while I don't want people taking in money they claimed would go the Project 'A' then instead diverting it to Project 'B', I'd expect they'd feel a sense of partnership with the generous people who reach out in good will to help them. If you've been too blessed, consider other Good Samaritans to point donors toward.

Hidden Benefactors

Some people seem to take a great delight in hating the wealthy. I see this behavior as being in conflict with some of my personal views and don't feel I have the time left in this life, or the right, to hate anybody for what they've accumulated. Besides, it's such a waste of such a strong emotion. What I especially like about the wealthy is the surprising number of them who come from impoverished circumstances and have an especially, though often hidden from the public, generous side. I only recall ever personally meeting one billionaire and he was dressed so shabbily at the time I felt sorry for the man, not knowing who he was. However,

I've met dozens of millionaires, many of them worth hundreds of millions. What I've found is most of them are incredibly likable and more generous with giving to charities than the average person would ever expect.

As a wary Samaritan the only times I've ever personally seen million-dollar gifts come to charities that I was affiliated with, they came from wealthy men and women. The only time I've ever seen billion-dollar gifts to any charities, they came from incredibly wealthy men and women. I regularly receive challenge letters from different charities I support, each telling me they've received a promise of a matching gift. It goes something to the effect of "For every dollar you send, the anonymous benefactor(s) will match your dollar." I love this and always try to help, though certainly not at the million or billion dollar level. For better or worse, this is a capitalistic system we live in here in The United States of America. I applaud people who are giving millions or billions away, even if they hold onto a few millions or billions for themselves.

In all the 45 years I've fund raised, I've never seen wealthy benefactors appreciated as much as they should be. Simultaneously, I've rarely encountered a wealthy benefactor who wanted a big deal made of their often incredibly generous efforts, efforts which they downplay or even hide from the entire world.

How We Come To Be Wary Samaritans

The first sign your wary Samaritanism is about to get a try out is when your wife asks you to help the husband of someone she knows, in a small business deal. You're informed they also don't speak English well. The wife gives you a phone number and when you call it from your own number, no one will answer. Does this mean they aren't available? Does this mean the number is wrong? Does this mean they are filtering calls and don't recognize your number? In any event it's not a good sign. Still, you leave a message to get back to you and hope for the best. The friend calls back within 60 seconds and claims they just missed your call, but you're now confident they were listening to see if you were anyone they owed money.

Now we get down to the meat of the need for help. The friend lives 150 miles away, wants you to purchase a small piece of construction equipment locally for him, and he will come on the weekend to pick up said piece of equipment and pay you back the money you've been out. My wife rarely asks much of me so I agree to act as the go between and speak to the equipment owner. We finally connect, despite my wife's friend having the wrong name for the man. His actual name turns out to be Walter and my wife's friend's husband said his name was Steve. After a few minutes of conversation we both relax and agree on a time to meet the following day and the price he is asking.

The next day we make contact, I check out the equipment, it's in good shape and the $800 price is quite reasonable. We make a deal and exchange money and a receipt. I load the equipment onto the utility trailer I've brought along for just such an eventuality. I pull the trailer home and park it in my yard. I call my wife's friend and tell him the deal is done, he can come get his equipment. There is a moment of hesitation on the line and then he sets the hook, "Something's come up and I can't drive up there this weekend, do you suppose while you have it on your trailer you could drive it here to me in Los Angeles. I'll buy your gas." Now you may be chuckling to yourself in recognition, but how many of you are wary Samaritans because of just such incidents?

Too Much Analyses And Speculation
Being able to analyze the problems in our society and having the ability to speak about them intelligently does not assure us that those smart enough to do so will ever actually do anything more than analyze and have speaking ability. In fact these characteristics may be the indicators of a budding politician, preacher, or lawyer. A wary Samaritan is not always the most analytical or the most erudite person on the scene. However, a wary Samaritan can always be identified by their willingness to personally wade into the water while others stand on the shore and speculate as to its turbidity, temperature, and depth.

Action Speaks Louder Than Words
Don't you find the people who just go ahead and engage in a wary Samaritan life to be so much more refreshing than people who can only tell you about what they used to do, or what they're going to do when the time is right, or they finally get the perfect opportunity. It's been said ships can't sail on yesterday's wind and tomorrow isn't guaranteed to anyone. Those who spend their days in fear of getting involved, or are simply too slothful to get involved, or are waiting for the perfect moment to get involved will never have to worry about becoming a wary Samaritan.

Stand By Me
The idea we'd be better off individually if we simply disengaged from the world around us is a clear and present danger. Consequently we live in gated communities where the only time we're seen in the front yard is as we come and go from our employment or recreational activities. Forget knowing our whole neighborhood, many of us don't even know the people who

live in the houses on each side of us. We shop at markets miles from our homes, so we never get to know other people from our community because they too shop in markets miles from their homes. I could go on, but I know you could create your own list of similar examples of how we've become isolated in the midst of millions.

Here's the problem as I see it. Mankind has chosen to live in community for millennia because it's a lifestyle which works out well for almost everyone. Our modern world has deluded us into thinking we can be self-sufficient and without any need for other people. All the while our shared transportation systems, water systems, sewer systems, garbage systems, firefighting services and law enforcement needs say otherwise. Routinely, nature, current events, or both will come along with a severe storm, an earthquake, a hurricane, a riot, or a small war and suddenly we're right back where we started, huddled in the caves needing each other again. I raise this truth here for you to seriously consider; we need to know our neighbors or move somewhere we can.

I'm a wary Samaritan with good reason. I've had enough bad experiences with people in my life I'm cautious about how I approach life and how I engage other people. Simultaneously, I've not given up on life because of bad experiences and I've not ceased to engage other people because of having encountered bad people in the past. Many people today are preparing for scenarios like The End Of The World As We Know It (TEOTWAWKI) or Without Rule Of Law (WORL) as though they and their household will be able to stand off all the contrary forces they might face. I think this is a mistake and if it does happen people will die needlessly because of the idea they can exists as islands. Think about the lyrics to the old song, *Stand By Me*. Don't we all need someone to stand by us from time to time?

CHAPTER 6

Mildred Collins

Because I'm male, most of the Good Samaritans I recall reaching out to me as mentors were men. There were a couple of exceptions and I want to remember them in this book to you as another example of the positive impact a Good Samaritan can have in the life of a child. Sometimes the life of a child is a road side ditch. In this case she was my third-grade teacher at Myrtle Avenue School, in Lamont, California. Myrtle Avenue was and is a public school in an extremely poor farming community. Once Mrs. Collins finished her career there and 'retired', she worked with her Pastor to help establish a Christian school in the same community. Some of the younger members of my family would come to be taught by her decades after she taught me.

As I recall, Mrs. Collins (I still have trouble addressing my old teachers by their first names) was a member of the Cherokee nation, with long dark hair worn in braids wrapped on top of her head. She was quite an imposing figure to a child for both her appearance and her personal carriage. She was a non-nonsense, take no prisoners teacher of the type who once populated our public school system back in the days when we all left school knowing how to read, write, and do arithmetic. She was always firm, but fair and respectful of her students and would accept no less of them for herself or their fellow students. We knew she was a Christian because having no cafeteria at the school, we ate lunch at our desks and she always said grace each day until the state finally forbade it.

Mrs. Collins came from Oklahoma, as did my parents. Most of the children she taught in those days were the children of Okie migrant workers. If a teacher faces a similar crowd today they'd be expected to make all sorts of allowances for the deficits those children were experiencing in their homes (e.g., poverty, illiteracy, addictions, spousal abuse, child abuse, etc.). To the contrary, she was one of the most demanding teachers I ever had. She expected us to show up for school with any homework completed. She expected us to sit up straight in our chairs. She expected us to pay attention. She expected us to exhibit good speech. She expected us to exhibit good manners. She never asked more of us than she asked of herself.

I recall how often she would correct my speech; it was liberally mid-western accented and proper words were often replaced with their strained Okie versions. One of my major problems was saying the word "warsh" when I should have been saying 'wash'. I had several of these and struggled with this for quite a while. It didn't help that I'd developed a stutter in the second grade. One day after class was ending and the other children had gone she asked me to wait for a moment. When we were the only ones left she said, "Farrell, you're the smartest child in this class." I was stunned but before I could speak she went on. "But no matter how smart you are, in life people are going to judge you by how you speak and your manners."

"Right now you have problems with both." I started to drop my head in embarrassment and she caught me. "Don't do that. I'm neither angry nor am I ridiculing you. I'm your teacher and I want to be your friend." I was nearly in tears at this point with shame, but before I could cry she went on. "Tomorrow morning and every morning from now on through the end of the school year I want you to be at my home promptly twenty minutes before school starts. We'll walk to school together and I'll help you lose the stutter, learn to speak properly, and polish your manners. I can see your mother has worked on them already and we'll continue that." I didn't have any idea what to say. I felt like apologizing and when I started she stopped me. "Be at my house on Copper Avenue in the morning. You know where it is?" I shook my head and whispered, "Yes Ma'am."

For you who may wonder, we walked to school in those days and my house was about three-quarters of a mile North of the school. Mrs. Collins house was a block off the route and about five minutes from the school. When I arrived, expecting to head out for school, instead she invited me in and asked me to sit down. I sat down very cautiously on the sofa and looked around. I'd never been in a home so nice before at this point in my life. And while it wasn't a mansion, the furniture all matched, there was carpet on the floors, and everything which had a place was in its place. "You have a very nice house," I said, recalling something I'd heard a television character say.

She busied herself collecting her handbag, a book, and some folders and offered the book and folders to me. She kept the handbag and commented, "A gentleman always offers to carry things for a lady." She paused at the front door and upon noting my puzzlement said, "A gentleman always opens doors for a lady." I hurried around her to get the door and we were out onto the sidewalk and headed toward school. I don't recall what we studied that day, but when class was over I waited for her and asked if I could walk her home. She smiled as she replied, "Certainly." This began a daily ritual which lasted for the rest of the school year. By year's end I had all but lost the stutter, was speaking much less colloquially, and my manners were, if not impeccable, at least acceptable in polite society.

I was devastated when the school-year ended. The following year I had the very worst teacher I ever had in grade school. I learned years later she didn't like little boys and she was passing through menopause when I was in her class. By the spring of the year she took a 'medical leave' and I never saw her again. I won't mention her name here, though fifty-two years later it's still burned in my mind, along with many of the insults and indignities I bore at her hands. I have to wonder if Mrs. Collins hadn't taken me under her wing if I could've come through my fourth grade year without a permanent stutter and a hatred for schools and learning. Instead I bore it as best I could and my fifth grade year I was blessed with another wonderful teacher, Barbara Johnson.

Mrs. Collins is long gone to her eternal reward. She taught thousands of children over a very long career in education. I'm unsure what she meant to her other students, but for me she was a turning point in my life. She taught me a little bit each day in those walks, not so much by what she lectured, but by her living example. Her rescue of me didn't happen in a one-time encounter where she found me injured on the roadside, bound my wounds, provided me transport, and deposited me at a nearby Inn. Her rescue of me took five days a week with a little bit of her day in the morning and a little bit in the afternoon. I think of this often when I work with youngsters when their energy or ignorance tires me. Her memories compel me on...

Miracles Are Within Your Power

Let's not limit our Good Samaritan efforts to crises. A wary Samaritan doesn't have to limit herself to only reaching out to others in the most dire moments in life; she can be just as useful to others by making efforts as simple as helping someone experience the fulfillment of a lifelong dream. Think of all the people out there today who openly admit they have a bucket list of unfulfilled dreams they want to complete. It ranges from people wanting to skydive to people wanting to visit the Great Wall of China to people wanting to complete a college Algebra class so they can get a degree.

My point here is being a wary Samaritan shouldn't just be about rescuing folks who've been robbed, beaten, and left in the ditch. It should also be about making the world in general a happier and better place. Certainly reaching out to folks in a moment of extreme need carries out the highest ideals of the Good Samaritan ethos, but the often unspoken needs associated with unfulfilled dreams can at times be just as important to an individual as medicine, food, or drink. I encourage you to listen to your friends, relatives, and business associates and see what miracles may well be within your wary Samaritan powers to bring to reality.

Improving Your Wary Samaritan Perception

Upon close consideration I find it's often harder for me to spot positive examples of human behavior than it is to spot negative examples. This may well be because I've become attuned to the negative aspects of human behavior because it has such immediate power to harm me or those I love. Consequently, as an act of self-preservation I've become expert at spotting negative human behavior quickly. As a fellow wary Samaritan, I suspect many of you are as hypervigilant in this area as I am. The result of this mindset is the negative behaviors and their associated danger catches your and my eyes first. This doesn't make us evil people, but it does say we've likely earned the wary moniker through previous bad experiences.

Ironically, one of the most positive things to have come out of me writing this book is it's having forced me over the past couple of years to look harder each day for the good things people do and not to focus so much on the bad things people do. I find I'm less critical as a result as to what constitutes a good work now and much more willing to impute good motives and assessments to people for their efforts than I might've been in the past. Give it a try. Make a point of looking for more good deeds in the world in the coming weeks and see if you can't spot more of them too. Furthermore, consider re-evaluating your judgements of other people's acts to see if there isn't a more positive lens through which they could be viewed.

In Luke's Gospel it says, "Unto whomsoever much is given, of him shall be much required." If you're one of those people this passage was being directed to, the burden seems to clearly fall to the smart person, the gifted person, or the person who's been blessed with life's tangible goods. If you are one of those people you might want to lighten up on those around you who may not be quite so smart, quite so gifted, or quite so financially blessed. Yes, among Good Samaritans there'll be superstars whose names will be known and whose faces will be instantly recognized. Never allow the idea to become imbedded in your thinking that the majority of good works are carried out by those superstars.

The truth is it's the Good Samaritan of average or lesser abilities who step up most often.

Volunteer's Remorse

As a wary Samaritan you already know what volunteer's remorse is. It's just like buyer's remorse except it involves those times when you as a Good Samaritan have let your heart get in front of your head once again. Sometimes the remorse hits you almost immediately and other times it only sets in days later when the magnitude of what's actually involved in fulfilling your promise becomes clear.

Wary Samaritans can become weary Samaritans simply because they take on too much. If you're one of those people, you'll likely have to be steamrolled by the magnitude of your volunteering many times before you finally wise up and start to pick your battles. Until then, all the rest of us can do is pray for you and hope you learn your lesson in this area before you physically or mentally break down.

Too Wary A Good Samaritan

A man in the parking lot of a Southern California McDonald's® today made a Good Samaritan gesture toward me and at first I ignored it, being the wary Samaritan I am. He offered some advice on the trailer I was towing and I nodded politely, but went on inside without taking it to heart. In the course of the ten minutes I was inside McDonald's® getting a burger and a drink, it hit me this man had attempted to do me a kindness and I'd dismissed it.

When I came back out, the man was still sitting in his truck and so I made a point to walk up to the window and apologize for my dismissiveness. Then I thanked him for trying to be of help me. Next I admitted this was the first time I'd owned this particular style of trailer and his advice on a safety item on it was outside the realm of my knowledge. I forced myself to go through this apology and admission because when we're arrogant or dismissive of others we need to recognize what's happened and nip such attitudes in the bud. I made the correction he suggested before I drove away and was glad I'd both apologized and taken his advice.

Wary Samaritans must be careful we don't become calloused by life's less than positive encounters. Otherwise we become suspicious of everything and everybody. I like to remind myself and others we're wary Samaritans not paranoid Samaritans. I've cautioned audiences over the years of our need to become neither scarred nor bitter, because either destroys our ability to be effective Good Samaritans. My mentor, John Sciford, warned me if men lost the sweetness in their souls then they've lost much of their ability to be of use to God. Nearly fifty years later, his wise and loving counsel is still sound.

Unexpected Good Samaritan

I had a fellow loan me a special trailer hitch this morning to pull a heavy generator mounted on a trailer. I needed to get the generator to project I was working on which needed portable power. He didn't have to loan it to me. He and I both knew I should have enquired beforehand to see what kind of hitch I'd need. It would've been well within his right to ignore the fact I didn't have the hitch I needed and simply direct me to the nearest merchant who could sell me one. This would of course have added time and expense to my day, but after all it was my own lack of foresight which placed me there.

Instead, he said the trailer company he worked for was fresh out of loaners, but he had his personal hitch on his own truck there in the parking lot he'd loan me if I'd bring it back later. It's rare for this wary Samaritan to be surprised by people, but this man surprised me with his kindness and then he told me where I could go later to buy one at the best price in town. When I dropped off the hitch in the evening, he wouldn't take any money for the use of his hitch and simply told me, "Just do something nice for someone in your life and I'll feel well paid." Every once in a while I too meet the unexpected Good Samaritan.

Go Easy On Yourself

Remind yourself often the work of a wary Samaritan is as little or as much as you want it to be. Some days you're more able and willing to reach out than others. This doesn't make you a bad person; it makes you a wise human being who's learned how to pick her battles. I've seen far more Good Samaritans burn out than wear out. It's for this reason I frequently remind fellow wary Samaritans to pace themselves; this is a marathon, not a sprint.

Unwelcome Warnings

I believe it's part of the work of a Good Samaritan to warn people of impending danger. Now immediately when I say this, some of you will begin to envision a wary Samaritan standing in the roadway in front of a washed out bridge, holding a lantern and waving arms frantically at approaching vehicles. This approach is all well and good and would certainly be a fine example. But more often than not the washed out bridge might be a potentially fatal decision a co-worker is about to make on the job, or a business investment being pursued by a loved one which your own experience tells you is doomed to fail, or a friend embarking on a personal relationship with a person you know to be a danger to your friend.

    I think you can come up with other examples of your own now as I've jarred your mindset. I'm not saying for you to become the family, workplace, or neighborhood busybody. What I'm saying is to always be concerned for the welfare of others and to have the courage to speak when others remain silent. I suspect many of us have had the experience of failing to speak up, only later to see a friend physically, financially, or romantically injured, or even killed. There are many kinds of danger and there many means you can use to warn others of impending danger. When we're admonished to be "…wise as serpents and harmless as doves" I believe this speaks to the need for wary Samaritans to exercise both wisdom and subtlety in their dealings.

Make Space For Others

Periodically we each see examples of the best in human nature, it rarely occurs in heavy traffic. I was in Los Angeles a couple of weeks back on business and chanced to be near the confluence of two great Freeways, the 210 and the 605. It was at the worst time of the day; late on a Friday afternoon. There were of course those individuals who refused to start to merge when their lane began to wane a mile or more back and waited until the last minute to force their way into the single combined lane. On the whole I was pleasantly surprised at how many people were being generous and allowing the cars in the right lane to have the space and time to merge into the single left lane. Moments like this do my heart good and give me hope for humankind. It also reminded me of how much life levels out if we work cooperatively.

Sometimes You Better Drive On Past

I came upon two young men in a late model car today who were pulled over at the side of a country road. Before I ever got near them I saw them in the distance trying to wave down passing vehicles. As I approached more closely they tried to wave me over as well. I was about to stop when my wary Samaritan sense kicked in. I chose to roll on past. I had a bad feeling seeing this newer car and two otherwise vigorous looking young men apparently stranded at the side of the road; It didn't compute.

Now I don't know for certain there was anything going on there other than two guys wanting someone to stop and help them. There was a time when you or I could've felt safe to offer assistance to almost anybody in a broke down car, but such a time passed 30 years back. I admit a twinge of guilt whenever this kind of encounter happens, but then every time I see where someone has been abducted, robbed, raped, or killed when they stopped to assist a stranded driver, my guilt goes right away.

Sharing Our Knowledge Is Sharing Ourselves

There are times in life when I ponder my youth, especially the years when I first began to be part of the workforce. I've always had a love for teaching and sharing the things I've learned and it's always puzzled me how many people I met over the years who were absolutely stingy about sharing what they knew in terms of skills and working knowledge. I recognize some of this is driven by fear of having someone you've trained take your job. But for many it goes far beyond basic fear and borders on the attitude of "I'm angry you want to know and think I'd care."

Good Samaritans, even a wary Samaritan, need to be reminded often how sharing ourselves and our knowledge may be the most giving thing we can do for other people. Our young people especially need those who are "...willing and apt to teach." A society breaks down without shared and received knowledge. I'm thankful for the men and women over the past forty-five years of my work life who shared their knowledge with me, allowing me to learn several trades, earn advanced degrees, provide for my family, and live long enough to share myself with others.

A Minute To Catch Your Breath

It never hurts my feelings when everybody is going out of their way to be safe, courteous, and concerned about others they encounter. Of course it can put a wary Samaritan out of a job on days when those things happen, but it thankfully provides a respite from the normal routine of shattered victims in the roadside ditch and allows us catch our breath.

A Wary Samaritan Knows No Holidays

As I write this, it's a national holiday here in the United States. Regardless of what country you may live in, it's the mundane events which take up the majority of our lives and even on holidays they continue unabated. Consequently, you might want to be on the lookout for opportunities where a wary Samaritan is needed. People traveling, playing baseball, swimming, boating, hiking, climbing, cooking, flying or parachuting all can have those moments when they truly need a helping hand. Go out and enjoy your holidays in whatever way you and your loved ones celebrate these kinds of events, but be willing to consider stepping into the ditch at a moment's notice if an unplanned catastrophe calls for it.

Children Need Good Samaritans Too

As you go about your day and you're paying attention to places you might bring some light in the darkness, consider the lives of your neighborhood children. I'm older and have more time these days to stop and talk with the neighborhood children than I ever would've had when I was young. The first few times I spoke with any of these kids I thought they were just listening to be polite. Later I thought out they might be listening because they found me amusing. Finally, I realized they were listening because here I was as an adult, speaking to them like they were adults too.

The conversations have ranged from what it was like to live in this house 50 years ago, to what kinds of vegetables and gourds I'm raising in this year's garden, to why a lizard's tail will grow back if it gets broken off while you're catching him. It's caused me to realize just as much as in my day, children want to be treated like adults. If we do this, surprisingly they'll behave in a more adult-like manner. I know young parents have their hands fuller now than ever and I know many grandkids, just like mine, live hours away from their own grandparents.

As a wary Samaritan, I'm even wary of children. Any relationship between you and someone else's child can be problematic, so always behave in an above reproach manner if you interact with the kids in your neighborhood, or any kids for that matter. You don't have to become the person always handing out snacks to the local kids; I think more of them crave the one-on-one recognition and attention than a cookie anyway. I hear many voices complaining about the state of our children. Here's your opportunity to start being a positive role model to help change the next generation.

The Need At Hand

In our rush to do good works for others, we can easily overlook those closest to us; our family and friends. Think about it this week as you go about your wary Samaritan life and see if you can find an opportunity to help a family member or friend. There's really no constant need to be out scouring the roadside ditches for opportunities to serve others when there may well be folks in need of a Good Samaritan right inside your family or circle of friends.

Wary Samaritan Sense

I was in the hardware store this afternoon and happened to be searching for electrical breakers in close proximity to a fellow who was a bit too full of himself as he made a point of proclaiming about every sixty seconds he didn't know why they didn't get a clerk over there to help him. After all, he was in a huge hurry and they were wrecking his afternoon. I heard his female companion try several times to calm him down and to point out how calmly I was waiting. I moved off a few feet more when she said this out of fear I'd get drawn into their little drama. The female went off to search for the clerk and in a couple of moments I heard another call over the public address system for a clerk to come to the electrical department immediately. Three or four minutes later the female companion and the electrical department clerk came up together.

Mr. You're Ruining My Day immediately began to berate the slow service. The clerk took it all in and did her best to get this fellow the breaker he told her he needed. It cost $114 due to the brand being nearly obsolete. He ranted and raved about the price, then grabbed it from her hand and hurried away. At such a price it had been previously locked away. As she was relocking the case, I said, "You know, that wasn't the breaker he needed." She smiled and said, "Yes, but if you heard him he wouldn't let me get a word in edgewise and insisted it was the one he wanted. Besides, I get off in 15 minutes and I'm off for the next three days. Any way, if it was wrong why didn't you speak up?" I smiled in understanding because as much as I wanted to help this man find his breaker, calm him down, and have a pleasant day, my wary Samaritan sense was putting out a high danger warning signal and I wisely kept quiet.

Must I Fight You To Help You

I have a philosophy about helping other people which took me about 45 years to arrive at. What pearls of wisdom are entailed in this philosophy gained after 45 years as a wary Samaritan? It's simple really; I shouldn't have to fight with you to help you. In fact, no one should have to fight with anyone in order to help them. Now I know immediately some of you are picturing scenarios in your mind's eye of situations where in order to help people you might have to fight with them. Good for you! I say go for it with all the gusto you can muster. You're clearly a better person than I am and much more filled with compassion than I am. The world needs people like you because if they live long enough they'll become people like me.

Here's where I can't embrace the "beat me up" approach anymore, and why I can't champion it for anyone else either. Across a lifetime I've found that people who fight with you as you try to help them are not going to benefit from your help in the long term and you'll be back there fighting to help them again and again. I've learned sometimes it's more effective to let fate take its course with them and offer help at a later date when the fight has gone out of them. You can do as you please, but as I age I only have a certain amount of time, energy, and money to devote to Good Samaritanism. What I don't have is any more time, energy, or money to fight with people in order to force a solution to their problems on them. I shouldn't have to and you shouldn't either.

Searching For The Fire

As the years have gone by I take a more studied approach to everything I engage in, especially the role of wary Samaritan. Where I used to see crisis as the only legitimate place for Good Samaritanly acts, I now recognize every situation requiring a Good Samaritan isn't already on fire and needing to be dealt with right this instant. By slowing down, I've further realized there were a lot of places in the past where I could've been of real value. I missed them because I was searching for the fire instead of looking for places I could've prevented a fire.

I must now admit embarrassedly so many of the fires I would later fight started out from situations I'd previously been in too much of a hurry to see. I regret there were times I could've prevented the need for full-blown wary Samaritan involvement if I'd just dealt with the minor issue I passed by, while it was only a spark. All Good Samaritans might be better served if we spent more time sorting out the details and potential future ramifications, than to ignore minor problems until they reach critical mass. It's not as heroic, but if heroics are your motivation, you're in the wrong business.

Babysitting Good Samaritans

I attended a party over the weekend. While I sat there among the 'old people', many of them offered to keep an eye on the younger parents' children. It came to me this act of the older people offering to watch the younger peoples' toddlers at events of this sort is an admirable act of Good Samaritanism. Today many young couples have small children, and the grandparents, aunts, uncles, and cousins on both sides are a thousand miles away. Being able to visit, laugh, dance, play volleyball, and enjoy the diversion of an event can be a huge relief to young moms and dads who never have enough minutes in their week at this stage of their lives. So even if you're a wary Samaritan, here's a place where your kindness can make a difference in someone's life and for the most part you can do it while sitting and only occasionally having to get up and chase the little guys.

From One Fire To The Next

While I'm on the theme of fighting fires let me reaffirm I've had times in my life when it seemed like I was just moving from one fire to the next. I would no sooner get an issue resolved at one location, when almost immediately word came there was a crisis at another location. I finally realized if I allowed myself to be hurried from crisis to crisis, this wary Samaritan would one day simply be a dead Samaritan. Some of us Good Samaritans, me included, have had to learn to attach only the significance necessary to each new problem we encounter. Not every need is a matter of life and death and a Good Samaritan should judge each need on its own merits.

I know Good Samaritans who see every encounter as a life or death matter. Accordingly, their stress levels stay sky high 24/7/365. This doesn't help the Good Samaritan, this doesn't help the people he or she will eventually encounter, it does burn out the Good Samaritan, and assures a valuable human resource will no longer be available. You have to ask yourself if you can run all out in every instance for the rest of your shortened life, or if perhaps you could pick and choose to only inject yourself in the places you're most needed and most capable of being of help. High blood pressure, heart attack, chronic anxiety, and a host of other maladies accompany this constantly being in fight or flight mode.

Crashing And Repairing Your Hard Drive

I've mentioned somewhere in this book how I began replacing a Hard Disk Drive in one of my desktop personal computers recently. Today I reinstalled the last of the software and my backed up files to get me back to square one. As I was doing all of this I realized I could make corrections to the program set ups and hardware along the way. By corrections I mean the errors or downright mistakes I'd made when I installed software or hardware over the last three or four years could now be corrected. It suddenly seemed very liberating and not nearly so tedious when I took the frame of mind I could make some gains out of what has for a ten-day period seemed like one loss after another.

Then it hit me that from time to time in my life when I've suffered a personal crash of one sort or another, I'd felt this same sort of elation I felt upon realizing my computer could be 'better' than it was before. Many times as I've literally lay recovering, I've realized I could make some changes so the new me would be an improved version when compared to the old me. It's a sad commentary I often have to crash before I'll change a malfunctioning life. Yet there it is. Make of it what you will, but I'd like to think I'll do better in the self-initiated change department going forward. Realistically, having closed out six decades, I am who I am. For those of you who are less stubborn than me, I hear

God's mercies are new every morning and any day is a good day to make a necessary change.

What Compels You
There is no better feeling for a wary Samaritan than to reach out to help someone and then be able to see both how it changed their life and the genuine gratitude they have for what you've done. I was going over all the reasons in my mind earlier today which compel people to be Good Samaritans. I checked off religion, philosophy, childhood training, extra credit assignments, even Boy and Girl Scouting. But after a while I still couldn't come up with any reason better than getting to see peoples' lives changed for the better and their genuine gratitude. Sometimes you see changed lives, sometimes you see gratitude. But seeing the combination of those two in the same person is priceless. You can't build your efforts in expectation of one or the other or both, but you can certainly enjoy them when it happens.

Be Aware, Stay Aware
Being a wary Samaritan gives me a different perspective on life and sadly it's not always a cheery one. We were exiting the freeway tonight and as we approached the top of the off-ramp, the light was green. At the limit line of the intersection the driver of the car ahead of me suddenly came to a full stop in order to hand a bill to someone with a hungry & homeless placard. I diligently braked and barely avoided a collision. The BMW behind had seen the green light, but not the fact I had a car ahead of me. If the beamer driver hadn't swerved out at the last instant, the hungry and homeless guy, my wife and me, and the benefactor would've all been headed to the ER. People, I love a Good Samaritan as much as anybody does, but for God's sake exercise

some discretion and don't get yourself or someone else killed or injured doing something similar to this. It's never a good deed when you cause a multi-car accident, no matter how noble your initial efforts may have seemed.

Kindness Today

When you consider all the things you could do as a wary Samaritan to make the world a better place, never short change the simple idea of kindness. We live in an increasingly brutal world where rough and tumble is the status quo ante. So when you break the mold by behaving kindly, it will at first startle people who've become used to receiving harsh or outright brutish treatment at every turn. As you continue to behave with kindness, it releases the spirit of kindness into the world; it's a spirit which is infectious, and capable of leading countless others to similar acts of kindness. Why not try it today!

Practitioners Of Personal Evil

Every once in a while I encounter someone who seems to relish their own evil. By this I mean whereas a wary Samaritan goes through life searching for moments where we can reach out and do good for others, there are those who seem to be searching for moments in life where they can hurt, discourage, or even destroy someone. Some would say it's the product of a mental illness or a bad childhood and seek to excuse such behavior. My mother would've said they were just going through life hurting people and being evil. She'd have said they needed to repent. Sometimes they're total strangers, sometimes they're acquaintances, and unfortunately sometimes they're your relatives. These kinds of people are all good reasons to stay wary out there.

Works Of Faith

There's an ideal place and time for wary Samaritans to engage in our Good Samaritanism. Conversely there's an ideal place and time to disengage from it. However, an even better approach, which can admittedly take years to master, is to learn to entirely avoid some engagements in the first place. The ability to know which time is at hand is what makes the difference between fruitlessly going through the Good Samaritan motions and life-changing God-directed works of faith. I remind folks in business management almost constantly of the need to pick their battles. The same advice can certainly be offered to Good Samaritans everywhere with regard to works of faith. Pick your battles or your battles will pick you to pieces.

Heart Of A Good Samaritan

As a wary Samaritan I'm always encouraged when I read or hear in the news about someone who's successfully gone out of their way to help another person, especially if it's a total stranger they help. This week there were a couple of these events which were called to my attention, but one stood out to me because it involved saving the life of a young child who'd somehow managed to get out of an upper story window and roll onto a window awning many feet above the ground. The man credited with getting involved and saving this child's life was just a passerby who saw a tragedy unfolding and decided to inject himself into the situation. He had absolutely no legal duty to step in.

Jesus is said to have told those who were listening to him teach one day that it's an easy matter to help our friends or family, but an altogether different matter to reach out to strangers. Jesus reminded his listeners they could almost always expect reciprocity from their family or friends for a good deed, but they didn't have a similar prospect of a returned favor from a stranger or an enemy. This is where altruism comes into play for the wary Samaritan. As usual, I urge caution when you're out there, but not so much you abandon a world and its people while it's in such a terrible state of need. I believe most of us want to do good. Yes, sin is always present in each of us, and yet the overwhelming majority still wants to do good. Go with the urge to do good.

Justice Cometh And That Right Soon

I had an English teacher in high school who often used the phrase, "Man's inhumanity to man" when he sought to make a point about how cruel human beings can be to one another. The English teacher is long dead but the phrase lingers on in my mind and comes immediately to the fore when I hear of some new incident where one human being has inflicted unnecessary cruelty or death on another.

Today, it was the tale of a boardinghouse landlady who'd been in a feud with a local businesswoman for some time. The landlady suddenly demanded a tenant vacate the premises because she'd heard of the success of her nemesis, the tenant's employer, and how the tenant had contributed to the employer's success. She calculated that if she put the employee on the street, the employee would then be forced to leave the area and her job and in turn her employer would suffer loss.

Now in this case, the employee (with her employer's help) was quickly able to find a new rental and life rolled on even better than it had before. But picture a woman having such a bitter spirit toward the success of the woman's business rival that she'd exact her retribution on a hapless employee who was simply trying to make a living. This behavior is as inhuman and cowardly as it is unlawful.

Legal considerations aside, what this landlady did is a clear example of man's inhumanity to man, or in this case woman's inhumanity to woman. For the course of a day she threw this poor woman's life into disarray by putting her out on the street on an hour's notice. Imagine how you'd feel. Just when this wary Samaritan thinks he's heard it all, some new iteration of another of the most disgusting aspects of human behavior crops up and I'm surprised again.

All major religions have some sacred scripture which addresses how the almighty feels about people mistreating the poor, the weak, or the powerless. Just as surely, all of them have some sacred scripture which talks about the what goes around comes around, reaping and sowing, or Karma. My suspicion is this malefactor's day is coming. The unknown here is just how many people she'll treat this way before her comeuppance. Once again I'll remind you bitterness does more damage to the bearer than the victim it's directed toward.

Unhappy Needy People

Being a wary Samaritan is never easy, but there's very rarely a dull moment in life when it comes to trying to perform good deeds. I find it only slightly amusing how often in life, "No good deed goes unpunished." I'm sure some of you who've read my blog, *TheWarySamaritan,* know the man who wrote it has had his share of unappreciated effort. But just like Charley Brown, I keep trying to kick the football Lucy offers up; I keep thinking things will turn around.

There was the time I offered to adjust a clutch for a young man for free because he was unemployed and needed his vehicle to find work, only to discover all the adjustment was used up and the guy actually needed to think about a new clutch. He was angry with me because his friends had assured him the clutch could be adjusted. Where were these friends now while my knuckles were busted, my hands were greasy, and I should've been home eating Sunday dinner with my wife and kids?

Another time there was the woman who contacted me as a contractor because she badly needed a roof repair. Seeing she was a single mom I offered to make the repair entirely at my cost for the materials and not charge her for my labor. I personally felt like this was a generous offer. She, on the other hand, was offended and said the cost wasn't cheap enough and I'd need to lower my price. Presumably I was supposed to provide the materials as a gift! Free labor alone wasn't enough and now I was a bad man because I wouldn't donate both labor and material.

However, my favorite example was helping a failing graduate business student rework an absolutely terrible organizational theory paper for another professor, then having the grad student return to me angry when he only got a letter grade of 'B'. Imagine how shocked I was at his upset since I was expecting some word of thanks for pulling him out of the fire. I suppose I could've written it entirely for him, but I erroneously figured he might actually want to learn something for himself; silly me!

You'd think wary Samaritans would've learned long ago some people would rather be unhappy, would rather be lied to, or would rather be damaged by avoiding the truth than to take personal responsibility for their own world and graciously accept whatever helping hands are offered them. Moreover, you'd think they'd do so without berating those offering the helping hand? I don't think there's any danger of wary Samaritans ceasing to exist any time soon. Unhappy needy people are a natural constant and will pop up along every Good Samaritan's road from time to time, thus assuring more wariness out there.

Giving Just A Little

There was a wonderful health care commercial on the radio this morning extolling the benefits of sharing the roads. It went on to talk about some of the practices I've advocated over the years regarding how well the freeways function when people will give a little and share the road. The commercial extrapolated this concept and talked about what a different world it would be if we could expand the practice of giving a little. That's music to the ears of every wary Samaritan... and anyone who dislikes discourteous drivers.

Never Judge Another Wary Samaritan

Your Good Samaritan behavior is determined to large degree by your inherent abilities and resources. By this I mean your ability to do good works is constrained by your time, finances, intellect, physical and mental health, and so forth. I see other wary Samaritans who are graced with more or less time than me, more or less financial resources than me, more or less intellect than me, and more or less physical or mental health than me. I know the previous sentence became repetitive, but I wanted to grind the point home how all wary Samaritans aren't created equal.

Consequently, for as long as you live, those around you will express their Good Samaritanism in ways which fit in with their life, their generation, and their means. Some good advice here would be to never judge another wary Samaritan. Don't be jealous of another wary Samaritan because they're able to do more. Don't look down upon another wary Samaritan because they're able to do less. After all, who are you to judge whether it was more or less? Instead, be happy good deeds are done and leave it to God to sort out all the rest of the details. Romans 14 mentions how a person is accountable to his own master, not to you, and not to public opinion.

An Inconvenient Time
There are days when wary Samaritans are out searching for good deeds to do and no situation in need of a Good Samaritan can be found. At other times there are days on which a wary Samaritan has a million things needing to be done and not enough time to do them; suddenly need seems to be everywhere? I find when I have free time there may indeed be no need at hand. Conversely, I find when I am overloaded, needs pop up like weeds in the springtime. I've concluded repeatedly, and am reminded of it routinely, how need seems to always come along at an inconvenient time; if you would be a wary Samaritan, get used to it.

Con Artists Of Every Stripe
Professional people and health care workers scamming other people makes me furious because they're betraying a positon of trust. I don't care if it's politicians, televangelists, physicians, funeral directors, lawyers, accountants, nurses, social workers, or pharmacists. I have no use for anyone who uses such a positon to steal the money and the dignity of our most at risk citizens. Unfortunately, their thieving numbers seem to be constantly on the rise as evidenced by a steady stream of reports in the media and those I hear privately from other professionals.

There's a huge amount of need in the world and I've been either blessed or cursed, depending on your point of view, to have seen a good deal of it on four continents. Sadly, it's not limited to the developed world; it can be seen almost anywhere. When I encounter people who are scamming at-risk fellow citizens for a buck while pretending to help them, or are falsely claiming a dire personal need in order to drain someone else's bank account, it sets my teeth on edge. This is a cruel and calculated misuse of other people's better nature. This abuse damages both their bank accounts and their outlook.

As each of you knows, a wary Samaritan is wary with good reason. I see critical financial resources going into the hands of con artists of every stripe, while the women, children, and elderly they steal them from remain in dire need. I see people selling hope to the hopeless where all which is really for sale is an illusion concocted to facilitate thievery. I pray there's a special place in Hell for these human parasites. I urge you to do all within your power not to be taken in by them, or to allow those you care for to be taken in by them either. The rise of social media seems to have only made the situation worse.

Beyond this familial vigilance, be on the lookout for them in your own neighborhood and don't be shy to contact legal authorities when it's obvious the aged, the ill, children, or the mentally incompetent are being taken advantage of by those who may claim to care for them the most. In the late nineteen nineties I spent a little over a year administering a program where we investigated these kinds of evil acts upon senior citizens and those adults who were adjudged to be mentally incompetent. I can tell you often all it took to break the cycle of thievery and abuse was a phone call to the proper authorities. Even a wary Samaritan can, and should, make these kinds of phone calls.

Bad Samaritans

Throughout this book I talk about the people out there scamming the public by claiming a need while in fact they're merely clever con artists. I suspect you'll see and recognize some today as you go about your business. Interestingly, I was reminded over the weekend of a similar problem which takes on more of a wolf in sheep's clothing approach. They're an equal if not more difficult problem than the con artist/beggar. I refer to them the "Bad Samaritans" along the road side.

Believe it or not there are people who pose as Good Samaritans in order to gain access to otherwise cautious but suddenly vulnerable victims. It happens at accident scenes, it happens in health care settings, it happens with nurses and nannies, and it happens at churches, synagogues, and temples. In fact, it happens just about any place where people are vulnerable through a momentary or long-term need for help. It can easily happen to you or a loved one. This is possible because when we're in a state of personal danger, ill health, or injury, many of our natural defenses are down.

Bad Samaritans have been known to steal auto accident victim's possessions while pretending to be there to help. Bad Samaritans have been known to steal the possessions of people in hospitals and nursing homes while pretending to be there to help. Bad Samaritans have been known to rob other parishioners while they pretend to be there to help. In fact, if you can name a helping situation I'd make the certain bet someone has illegally exploited it for their personal gain, and more than once. The more at need or trusting we are the more vulnerable we become too Bad Samaritans

The hardest part here is sometimes they're the people we're taught to trust as children or we're forced to trust due to the expediency of the situation we're in. Emergency personnel, nurses, therapists, law enforcement officers, social workers, and medical attendants have all been caught being bad Samaritans. Physicians, lawyers, and accountants too, have been found to be using their 'Good Samaritan Guise' as a cover for bad Samaritan activities. The media is filled with such stories.

If you, a friend, or a loved one are approached in a moment of need by what on the surface appears to be a Good Samaritan, think about these words from this wary Samaritan and keep your eyes and ears open. The old admonishment to trust but verify never hurt anyone and in cases like these any good done for you will be far outweighed by the evil perpetrated upon you. Other wary Samaritans out there can help by keeping their eyes and ears open so they're able to expose these thieves for what they are any time they encounter them.

A final word of caution now if I may. It's best to rely upon professionals in law enforcement, child protective services, or adult protective services to confront these people. Just because you can identify them doesn't mean you're capable of handling the problems they can produce or the evil or injury they can generate. They can be incredibly intelligent, even sociopathically so. This makes them both smart and highly dangerous. I'd go so far as to say most, if not all, will claim you're mistaken and even try to reverse the charge by claiming you're the bad actor. Be wary out there and protect yourself, your loved ones, and your neighbors at all times.

Keep Your Heart Open To Children
It hit me again today that if there ever was a group which regularly needed a wary Samaritan working in their behalf, it would be

children. I grew up poor in a poor neighborhood and know well the deprivations the children of the poor deal with. But the fact is I've seen children from neighborhoods with million dollar homes who needed a Good Samaritan or two on their side just as much. Regardless of what neighborhood or socioeconomic class you come from, there are children around you in need. Some need a cookie. Some need a friend. Some need help with their math. Some need a champion who will report they're being abused.

Whatever it is they need, you could be their Good Samaritan. Yes, it does take a willingness to engage in the rough and tumble of life. You can't stand on the sidelines of life with all the other spectators and simultaneously claim to be in the game. Each of us older folks routinely come in contact with children. It could be in your neighborhood, it could be at your house of worship, or it could be a random encounter at the local market. A wary Samaritan is not a blind Samaritan. Keep both your eyes and your heart open to the needs around you... and certainly don't overlook the needs of children.

Give It Away

Like most Americans, this wary Samaritan has accumulated a lot of possessions, my kids would say junk, over the past six decades. In fact, I have items from my childhood back in the 1950s which only hold value for me. As my wife and I look at the years immediately ahead, we're both conscious of our own aging and our need to prepare for a smaller and less cluttered future. Many of our friends are already retired and have gone through their own downsizings, so we have some sense of what it looks like close up.

Many of them simply rented or built bigger storage rooms when they downsized from their existing too large house. I suppose the goal was to be able to dispose of these items in a slower manner, but truth be told they'll likely hang on until the end and their kids will have to deal with their lifetime of treasures at the mini-storage. When my parents were finally gone, even after my siblings had taken what they wanted, I hauled off more than ten pick-up truck loads to the landfill and enumerable loads to charities such as Goodwill and The Salvation Army.

Seeing this gargantuan labor I'd leave for the kids, and recognizing my own enormous volume of personal and business possessions, I've been deliberately looking at items with an eye toward who I know who might be able to make good use of them after I've gone. Now this doesn't mean I need to hang onto them until I die. In fact, what it means to me is I'm now trying to pass them along while I'm still around so if people need to know how something works, I can still teach them what I know. As we age you and I both have items we can never physically make use of again and in our heart we know it.

It occurs to me by doing this giving away; I can be a Good Samaritan on multiple levels. By giving others a tangible useful item and by simultaneously passing along my knowledge of its history, function, and how to use it, I can make a difference now and long after I'm gone. My generation is a transitioning generation which was born in the age of machines and lived to see the age of computers and artificial intelligence come into its own. Barring societal collapse, ours could be the last generation who built and operated machines instead of being controlled or made obsolete by machines.

CHAPTER 7

Are You Qualified

I originally wrote this passage to my grandchildren and it's been previously published in my book *In Your Time: A Twentieth Century Grandfather Writes To His Twenty-first Century Grandchildren*. This advice is so important, especially to all would-be Good Samaritans, I shamelessly include it here for you to consider. A Good Samaritan's bad advice played a role in the suicide of my only son. It was not the only role played there and I don't want to needlessly burden one player, but it can't be ignored and should stand as a caution to you. Here's the piece in its entirety.

> *I was reading an obituary yesterday and thinking about the bad advice people sometimes give. Most of the time advice is offered with the best of intentions and is meant to be genuinely helpful. Truthfully I think people may be way too liberal with offering advice in areas where they have nothing to offer but their opinions or things they've seen on the Internet. Unprofessional opinions can cause others great hardship, illness, injury, financial loss, and perhaps even death.*
>
> *Allow me to insert a word of caution at this point to you my children; our family does have a tendency to offer a lot of advice. If*

you should encounter people with serious mental, emotional, or physical challenges, you may want to tread lightly in the advice department. In my own time I've seen well-intentioned people offer advice or direction in situations where they really weren't qualified to comment at all and the outcome was disastrous. The death by suicide of your Uncle Ryan is an excellent example.

Ryan was under the care of both a psychiatrist and a psychologist; the turnaround in his mental health in the prior year had been remarkable. Ryan had put on weight, he was laughing, he was smiling, and he was enjoying life again. Enter a well-meaning but totally unqualified youth minister offering him the advice that if he would just discontinue his medications, God would heal him of his OCD, depression, and schizophrenic problems. As you know by now, it didn't work out too well.

This doesn't mean that people may not have a wealth of common sense and life experience to draw upon. But if common sense and life experiences were enough, there'd be no need for physicians, lawyers, psychiatrists, psychologists, accountants, and other professional advisers. It's okay to be a friend and it's okay to care deeply about people you know or meet. In fact if you care so deeply, you'll want people to receive the best in counsel.

Finally, it's not okay to ignorantly offer incorrect advice, no matter how well-intentioned. Sometimes the best a friend can do is to direct a friend to professional help.

Lizard Traps

I was looking out my window last evening and noticed the youngest son of my next door neighbor patrolling along the fence line between my place and theirs. I could tell by his furtive glances and the drinking glass in his hand he was engaged in a young boy's age old past time in my desert world; lizard hunting. I watched for two or three minutes and then decided to step out and speak to him. I'd spoken regularly with his two older brothers, but never with him. He was shocked by my silent appearance and his first attempt to respond told me immediately he was both shy and had some kind of speech impediment.

I ignored the shyness and the impediment altogether and behaved as though I'd just heard a response from some absolutely articulate person and proceeded to engage him in a conversation. I think he was so shocked I didn't just walk off when he stuttered that he began to pain-stakingly explain to me what he was doing. I stopped him after a bit! "I know exactly what you're doing... because I've done it myself along this very fence about this same time of the day, back when I was your age." He seemed genuinely shocked this portly gray-haired old man had ever been his age or ever hunted the wily Western Fence Lizard.

I immediately began to speak to him as one boy would to another and asked about how many he'd caught, if he'd seen any big ones, and if any of their tails came off. He was transformed at this and suddenly instead of halting speech and a fearful countenance it was one brave young hunter speaking to another old hunter about things they both completely understood. I asked him for his drinking glass and told him if he'd let me have it, I'd show him how to make a proper lizard trap, so he didn't have to chase the lizard. Truth be told, a beer or soda pop can works better but he had a drinking glass and a drinking glass would do.

The whole of this encounter was five minutes at most. I think I've gained a young friend who won't run away from the fence in the future (as he always did before) when he sees me come out in the yard. In any event he now has the fundamentals of how to trap lizards, versus chasing lizards. For you worry warts out there, I did explain to him a trap can become a cooker for a lizard in our area where it often exceeds 100 degrees Fahrenheit. He promised each time he set one he'd come check it often so he didn't kill any of our little scaly friends. Some days and in some circumstances a wary Samaritan must be less wary than others and engage where we would otherwise stand aside quietly unengaged.

Volunteer Opportunities

As surprising as it may seem, given my wariness, I'm a regular volunteer with a number of organizations which do good deeds. I've been volunteering for service of this sort since I was a cub scout, more than 50 years ago. Being a volunteer is a great way to be involved with a good work while at the same time not having to bear the whole burden of the good work alone.

There is a myriad of opportunities out there to volunteer and one of them is sure to fit your skills and mindset. Whether it's driving cancer patients to treatment, picking up litter along our nation's highways, serving meals at the homeless shelter, or tending the babies in the nursery at your house of faith, there are opportunities for just about any field and for as long or as short a period as you can offer.

Why not begin to think about volunteering if you want to be a Good Samaritan but have a little trepidation about launching off alone? By volunteering in this manner you get the chance to dip your toe in the water without being forced to immediately dive all the way in. If it turns out to be a good fit, you can fully engage, and if it doesn't fit you'll know more about yourself and where you need to go from there as a volunteer.

A Wary Samaritan At Home

As we age, social psychologists have noted we begin to withdraw from life over time. While it's certainly a normal part of aging, it's also posited one of the reasons for this is so sons, daughters, and grandchildren learn to count less and less on their parents and grandparents. In this manner they become fully independent by the time their parents and grandparents pass on. Even if all of this is true, and I have no reason to doubt it, this wary Samaritan feels certain we can continue to be a blessing to our families and those around us for as long as we're of sound mind. I specifically didn't say sound bodies, because many of us have begun to lose the sound body battle by the times we reach our 40s and 50s.

In Western culture we don't value our elders nearly so much as some other cultures do. Sometimes this is understandable and sometimes it's not. I find though if mom or dad, grandma or grandpa were not the most loving and caring people when they were younger, they may not be those kinds of people when they grow old either. This doesn't mean they can't change, turn over a new leaf, and become a blessing to their offspring. On the contrary, I've seen some amazing turnarounds as people hit their 50s, 60s, and 70s. What I'd suggest is aging is a time to evaluate how effective our life strategies have been and then use our assessment to help us decide if we want to continue them or change them.

Doesn't it seem hollow if we've been able in our lifetime to reach out to others, even to total strangers in their moment of need, but we are either unable or unwilling to do the same for those we love? I suspect the 50s, 60s, and 70s could be a time of mending fences as well as making personal reevaluations. As surprising as it is to some of us, and I count myself in this group, our children, grandchildren, and even great-grandchildren value us and want to be around us. They'll even put up with our foibles and cantankerousness to do so. It behooves each of us older Good Samaritans to meet them more than half way, because after all, we're the elders and should lead them by our example.

They say charity begins at home. I think it's an excellent aphorism and filled with truth on many levels. I'd say Good Samaritanism begins at home too! Yes, I know you're older, I know you're in declining health, and I know some of you live with pain all day every day. However, if you can find the time for your friends, if you can find the goodwill for your friends, or if you can find the ability to ignore the pain for your friends, why not do it for those you helped bring onto the planet? Being a Good Samaritan doesn't always mean you have to journey a thousand miles to do so. Sometimes a wary Samaritan is most needed at home.

Meeting Your Master's Expectations

At the risk of repeating myself, let me say each wary Samaritan encounters other Good Samaritans, who in his or her estimation are doing more or less than he or she is. When this happens in your journey, make a point to remind yourself not to judge them at all, and not to judge yourself too harshly. There's a scripture which I've shared in another place in this book about how a servant has to please has own master and not you. I see no place in the Good Samaritan's story of his having possessed a judgmental nature; apparently it's not part of the job description.

If this lack of a judgmental nature is true to the Good Samaritan, for us I believe it means whether our own master is pleased or displeased with us is all which really matters. Anybody else's opinion is not so important; opinions are like noses, everybody has one. So don't spend too much time in your life trying to decide whether or not you do too much or too little, or I do too much or too little in the area of good works. Instead, let's be concerned whether our own Master is satisfied with our individual efforts. You and I don't have to answer for anybody else.

Good Samaritans And Good Neighbors

Some people choose to live in the community where they have their habitation, some choose not to. By this I mean those in the latter group choose to live apart from the neighbors around them. They accomplish this by coming and going without ever knowing the names of the people in the next house or the next apartment. Remote controlled garage doors make it even easier to come and go while fully insulated by an automobile. I see it as being a Good Samaritan to foster community by working to create community. I know this sounds odd coming from a wary Samaritan.

I did half of my undergrad work in management and organizational development at a Mennonite University. I was 44 years old when I graduated from that institution and already had a lot of scars from many years of being a Good Samaritan. But during my time there I learned a great deal about the concept of community from the Mennonites and their Anabaptist perspective, which I'd seldom considered before. Presented against their backdrop of a sincere effort at New Testament living, it overcame my longstanding skepticism. Since then this wary Samaritan has believed being a good neighbor and being a Good Samaritan often covers a lot of the same territory.

Accepting The Good Samaritan

One of the most psychologically painful experiences I ever endured was to have to sit for ten minutes in a group session and have people point out my positive qualities. In fact, each of the fourteen members of the group had to endure the same thing. It turns out for most people it's very difficult to take a compliment without trying to divert it. I've concluded for many wary Samaritans it's much more difficult to accept a good deed done for us than it is to do a good deed for others. In my case, age and some physical debility has forced me to reconsider this thinking. My conclusion is I should've accepted peoples' willingness to help me a whole lot sooner.

I don't know about you, but it blesses me and lifts my spirits when I'm able to do something positive for someone else. This implies each time I've refused well-meaning help from some other wary Samaritan, I may not only have robbed them of their blessing related to giving, I may also have stopped them from performing an act which would've elevated their mood and personal sense of self-worth. Here's what I take away from this mental machination; don't be so quick to turn down people offering to do nice things for you. Your assumption these exchanges are all about you may be entirely erroneous, you may be creating a negative situation for both of you, where a win-win was intended.

Casting Bread Upon The Water

Have you ever done a good deed, never expecting anything of personal benefit to come of it, only to have some unexpected but related blessing come your way? This wary Samaritan has. From stories I've heard, so have many of you. I practice and teach the concept that good deeds should be done for their own sake and not with an eye toward "What's in this for me?" Regardless of where you stand on this philosophy, I often find unexpected blessing directly connected to some act of kindness I undertook a decade or more ago comes back to surprise and bless me today. So while I counsel you not to expect any kind of reward or recognition from those you reach out to help in a moment of need, I believe God has seen your good deed and never lets bread cast upon the waters fail to return multiplied one day.

More Than Enough Need To Go Around

Today as I looked around me and considered the amount and variety of needs in my daily world versus the number of Good Samaritans working to meet those needs, I was concerned we'll run out of our meager supply of Good Samaritans long before we exhaust our more than ample backlog of needs. Be a Good Samaritan, even if you must be a wary Samaritan to do so.

Prepared To Be A Good Samaritan

In thinking about Jesus' story of the Good Samaritan the other day it occurred to me I'd overlooked a critical fact in the overall makeup of this man. Specifically, the Good Samaritan was only able to give to the injured man those things which he already possessed. Now at first this seemed like such a trivial matter to me I almost overlooked it again. It's not trivial or superficial at all. In fact, it's key to the work of all Good Samaritans. You can only give to those who are in need, those things which you already possess.

I've pointed out previously in my writings that each Good Samaritan, including this wary Samaritan, is constrained in some way (e.g., finances, education, time, etc.). It struck me the original Good Samaritan already possessed things like concern, compassion, empathy, and the ability to bind up wounds. He also had transportation for the wounded man and he had money with which to pay for the man's care, food, and lodging. In short, this Good Samaritan brought a lot of positive qualities and tangible assets with him to the roadside that day.

This line of thought caused me to realize Good Samaritans are actually preparing for a catastrophe in a ditch long before they ever get there. It seems logical to me preparing to be a Good Samaritan is a lifetime effort which we undertake either consciously or unconsciously. I don't know if the original Good Samaritan had spent all his formative years readying himself for this one encounter or even imagining it would ever come. I do see the life he'd led before the fateful day had given him the exact set of resources he needed to be of assistance.

Arguably the life we live every day, with all of its mundane circumstances, shapes us into the people we'll become. The concerned become more concerned. The compassionate become more compassionate. The empathetic become more empathetic. Those with ability to bind up wounds become better at it over time. Each of these positive traits starts out as a small seed. If they're nurtured carefully, they'll grow into positive characteristics which help define our lives. If they're neglected, they wither and eventually die.

We've all seen people in which the seeds have died. They lack concern, they lack compassion, they lack empathy, and the idea of preparing a skill to be able to render help to others no longer enters their minds. They stand near the car wreck and gawk but never move to help. They yell to the suicidal, "Go ahead and jump." They drive past the fallen as they hurry to be about their important lives. The idea of giving their own money to charity to help feed the poor is an alien concept. They never prepared to be Good Samaritans and when the critical moment arrives, even if they were suddenly willing, they're rendered incapable by their own design.

Train Up A Child

During my childhood mother often worked three different jobs during to make ends meet. She'd become a maid at a hotel because the work was steady and year around, she worked in that trade faithfully for more than 25 years. But on the one day a week she had off, she cleaned other people's homes for extra money. Often she'd turn around and give money, food, or clothing to people she judged to have greater need than her own, all the while reminding my siblings and I we were better off than most of the people on the planet, though we certainly doubted it at the time.

I don't recall either my Mother or my Father lecturing us about how we should treat people who were down on their luck, hungry, in need of a job, or in need of a few dollars to buy bread and milk for their kids. What I do recall is watching them selflessly give to other people in need, stop to help people whose car had broken down, or lend money they'd saved for a washing machine to an old gambler so he could travel by bus to his only son's funeral in the East. My father also gave him his only suit, my mother gave him our only suitcase, and we drove him to the Greyhound station to see him safely off.

Now, let's look at the Old Testament verse again which I've used to entitle this passage. Notice it doesn't suggest we lecture a child in the way he should go. It doesn't say force a child in the way he should go. And it doesn't say get the school psychologist, the Congress, or one of his teachers to point out the way the child should go. It uses the word train. Training implies to me a concerted effort over some indefinite period of time until the training has taken hold in the life of the trainee. Training can be done by the written word, the spoken word, and visuals. Yet in this instance the more effective means seems to be by example.

You can't properly train a child through a series of scripted 60-second Public Service announcements. You definitely can't hope the leading actor or actress of the day will provide an example which will properly train your child. The training I've appreciated most has been when people trained me not with their lectures, but with their personal examples. I've always found it far easier to mimic a behavior if someone else can model it for me the first few times. In time, mimicking their model of behavior allows it to become second-nature to me. Consequently, I still prefer having an example initially; my parents were my first examples of Good Samaritanism.

My Father has been gone now for 20 years, my mother passed on almost eight years ago, and I'm getting old enough myself where I don't always recall the exact words my Mother or Daddy used in their training. What I do have are scenes which are permanently etched into my memory, scenes of my Mother or my Father reaching out to other people in need, powerful scenes which even an old wary Samaritan like me cannot dispel from his otherwise wary mind. So as you go along your way, be mindful of the example of Good Samaritanism you model for your children and your grandchildren; they are watching.

You Can't Take It With You

The way some people cling to every minute and every item in their lives, you'd think they're going to be able to take it with them when their time here on Earth comes to an end. One thing a wary Samaritan can take from archaeologists excavating those old tombs of the Pharaohs in Egypt is wherever grave robbers haven't already cleared out all of a Pharaoh's possessions, the archaeologists will. Your possessions will fall to others once your life is done. In some cases, you will have 'willed it so' and in other cases your possessions may in fact end up in hands you would not have wanted to hold them.

Consider what makes a life. Is it the things we've accumulated, the degrees behind our name, or the accolades others have heaped upon us? For some people this is all they have to show for a lifetime and having sat at the bedsides of many dying men and women, I've seen more than one bemoan the fact they pursued these "things" to the near-exclusion of all else. Some chose not to consider love and marriage. Some chose to love and marry but not to have children. Some chose to live lives of total self-absorption so they might attain those degrees, accolades, and celebrity status. When I later officiated at some of these funerals, they were often sparsely attended.

If you leave your children millions but you offered them a poor example of what constitutes a life, will they respect the money or squander it and hence squander your life's work? If you have an estate of fine homes, businesses, exclusive club memberships, and a portfolio of carefully selected stocks and bonds… can they fit in your urn or coffin? The time to consider these matters isn't while you're sharing your heart with a minister while lying on a bed from which you will never rise again under your own power, the time to consider these matters is now while you have a functioning mind and a functioning body. It's not too late to choose a different course.

Going With Grace
Occasionally you'll see a story in the news where some Good Samaritan has died while performing an act of kindness, which

we'd all recognize instantly as a very good deed. While this seems tragic, and it is, it appears to me this would be a far greater legacy to leave our children than to die wasting away in a nursing home bed or one of a hundred other ways in which one could pass on. Yes, I know we don't get to choose how we end our days.

It never hurts a wary Samaritan to be cautious, and I push the concept of caution all the time when I speak or write. Conversely, you can't live every minute of your life with such a high degree of caution you become a prisoner of your fears. So go ahead and perform those good deeds today, and if you should die in the doing, the rest of us will celebrate your life and the way you lived it. This isn't to say be reckless, but it is to say we must live, and sometimes die, with purpose.

Maybe They're The Crazy Ones

More than one person has suggested to me Good Samaritans are crazy. The critics stand on the outside looking in at another person who's acting on their empathy and reaching out to others in need. The critics often can't comprehend why anyone would do such things. It's timely here to note psychologists view a lack of empathy as one of the key signs of a narcissistic personality.

If you get enough other bad characteristics on the other psychological axes joining a lack of empathy, you're likely diagnosed as having strong narcissistic tendencies or even narcissistic personality disorder. This isn't a good diagnosis by any means! The harsh point this wary Samaritan is making is it may not be the Good Samaritans who are crazy after all; it may be some of their critics who need the mental health help.

This Isn't Dial-A-Prayer
In an earlier passage in this book I talked about a local church handing out a bag of goodies to people who are panhandling or asking for food. I had a friend tell me over the weekend he's had people begging for food reject bags of groceries when they were offered. He asked if I'd experienced this myself. I nodded my head affirmatively. I went on to tell him if people reject what I offer (e.g., food, money, roadside assistance, advice, medicine, etc.), I just move along and let it pass. Ironically, I've had some people do this and then ask for some alternative; usually the alternative is cash.

The way I view this is I offered them the best I had the first time, or at least the best I was willing to give away. I'm sure I'll encounter some other person in need, sooner or later, only too pleased to accept it. Being a wary Samaritan certainly doesn't mean being someone's doormat or giving them the right to treat you as if you're a concierge service. In similar situations it's been advised one shake the dust off one's shoes at these kinds of slights and move along to some place or some other person who's truly in need and willing to receive what's offered.

Inconvenient
Just to reiterate something you should already know, even if you have limited wary Samaritan leanings or experience. It will rarely be easy to reach out to people who genuinely need someone to reach out to them. It will come at the wrong time. It will come at the wrong place. It will come on the wrong date. It will come when you are not in a Good Samaritan frame of mind. And yet it's precisely at those times the need will manifest itself most often. It does make me wonder if it's some sort of test.

Donor Beware

Good Samaritans are easy marks! I say this because of some of the horror stories I've heard over the years where Good Samaritans were taken in by someone who assured them if they trusted the person, organization, or group with their financial assets, they could guarantee to double the money they'd have available to help other people in need. With most marks it's a case of their greed getting them taken in. With a Good Samaritan it's just the opposite; it's their desire to help the poor, diseased, lost, hungry, or lonely which gets them taken for a financial ride.

As I write this, I see summer nearing its unofficial end with Labor Day upon us; I know the holiday season is only weeks away. This is one of the key times of the year when professional con artists are at their busiest as they work to separate Good Samaritans from their hard earned money. My advice, be even more of a wary Samaritan during the last quarter of the year than you were in the first three. Be especially cautious of those who seem to know your donor history and your tax situation as well as you do. They may have already fooled you before.

I Could Learn To Live With It

I seem to have encountered so many people panhandling over my lifetime where now any time someone approaches me in a parking lot or in front of a store, I have the sinking feeling of "here we go again." Twice today people appeared to be approaching me in just such a manner and in both cases all I received from them was a greeting as they passed by. Sometimes a wary Samaritan is too wary and if it becomes the norm for people to be out wishing one another a great day instead of asking for change or food, I could learn to live with it...

Working The Lot

I could tell from two hundred feet out he was already targeting me. When I moved across the lane in the Walmart parking lot, he moved to the same side I did and continued to walk toward me. When he got about twenty feet from me he said, "My car's out of gas... can you spare a dollar?" I'm not sure what answers he'd gotten already, but mine must have been unexpected. When I said, "Show me your car and its gas gauge," he spit out a terse, "God bless you," and walked away in search of another less inquisitive benefactor. I would've helped him with some gas if he really was stranded; I've been stranded myself. However, I believe if he really needed gas he wouldn't have huffed off as he did. An hour later when I came out of the store, he was still working the lot.

Not A Heartless Samaritan

It never hurts to be the source of an encouraging word. I live in the community I was born in back in 1954. It was a community made up mostly of poor Okie farm laborers. I was raised to become a poor Okie farm laborer. Fate took a hand in my life and I went down another road. Yet I still feel at home here and no matter where I travel or have lived in the world, this little town is my home. It's changed only in the smallest way. Today it's a community made up largely of poor Hispanic farm laborers. I say Hispanic because Mexico, Puerto Rico, El Salvador, Nicaragua, and many points further south are all represented here these days. The other elephant in our community living room is the pervading knowledge as much as 40% of the people who live here are here illegally.

Now I'm not gonna jump off into political correctness and say they are undocumented, they are here illegally and I get it and they get it. Having said it, you need to understand the way I was raised is regardless of how you're here, you're a stranger in my country and God takes a real interest in how I treat you. So I don't go around asking for green cards if I see need. Tonight my washer has decided to die and I had to take a load of clothes to one of the Laundromats here in town. I washed two loads of towels and a young couple came in with two beautiful little boys who promptly sat down on a bench beside me while their parents set about loading washers and funneling in detergent and/or bleach.

They appeared to be around ages three and six. I took a medical interest; after all, I was a medical administrator for nearly a decade of my life. The older boy had pink eye; school just started here two weeks ago and school is a great breeding ground for infectious disease. Eventually I noticed the younger one had ring worm on his left forearm next to me. Now some of you at this point are disgusted and muttering about "...them damned illegals spreading disease among us." This kind of thinking never enters my mind when I see people who are sick, injured, or diseased. I think God expects more of me than dismissing obvious need he's sat down beside me. People what's wrong with us when we'll donate millions to missions and ignore the mission field at our door. I couldn't solve the immigration debate in a laundromat; I could direct them to help for their children.

I went over to Momma and Papa and in my best 'Spanglish' explained what was wrong. I saw their trepidation and knew many similarly situated young couples here would be rightfully concerned it's going to be an unpleasant conversation if an old Anglo is talking to them about their kids. Eventually we managed to communicate and I gave Momma directions to the local community health clinic. I told them how beautiful their little boys were and I told them I was once a poor farmworkers' child in this very town. I encouraged them to make their sons study hard and make a place for themselves here in America. You see, those two beautiful little boys are likely American citizens, and old codgers like me will need their skills and their taxes to live out our days. It's funny how community works this way.

A wary Samaritan should not be a heartless Samaritan.

CHAPTER 8

Ten Things The Good Samaritan Never Said

1. "Just look at the mess you've gotten yourself into."
2. "Can I call someone to come help you?"
3. "This wouldn't have happened if you'd travelled in a group."
4. "Who did you vote for in the last election?"
5. "You're causing me a lot of trouble and costing me a lot of money."
6. "If you'd been carrying concealed you could've driven away the bandits."
7. "Do you have any money hidden on you to help with your expenses?"
8. "Please stop bleeding on my best robe."
9. "What church do you attend? You sure don't look Baptist to me?"
10. "What were you thinking when you set out dressed like that?"

Fools Rush In

Where is it written a Good Samaritan must behave in a dangerous or foolish fashion? I encounter the mindset frequently which holds Good Samaritans have a duty to rush into situations where archangels fear to tread. Note I didn't just say angels there, I said archangels fear to tread.

Get a grip on yourself! Unless God has closed the mouths of lions for you already, you might not want to yell, "Bring on the fiery furnace," just yet. If he's closed the mouths of lions in your behalf, have at it. But until then, approach your efforts as a true wary Samaritan does, "with fear and trembling."

I read in the papers today where a young man decided to intervene in a fight outside a local nightclub in an effort to break it up. I think it's a noble desire. I also think it's one of those death wish approaches to life you'd best avoid. He's in the ICU and all the others involved are in jail or back at their regular lives.

So while I applaud his desire to do the right thing, this is one of those cases your Momma told you about where you have to really look things over closely and think things through clearly, before you rush in and risk life and limb. My sincere prayers are with him and his family.

Another Clever Idea For Good Samaritans

We've all been confronted by the beggar at the intersection or working their way through the grocery store parking lot, alternately asking for change while telling you they're hungry, homeless, or both. One of the local churches in my area is trying to do something about those scenarios other than just automatically saying no or mindlessly handing money to a total stranger. I'm not sure they're the originator of the idea, but it's a good one and worth a wary Samaritan considering.

They somehow came upon the idea of preparing hundreds of zip-lock bags with bottled water, granola bars, toiletries, and a gospel tract. Each member of the church was then asked to come and take as many as they felt they needed, with the promise they'd store them in their cars for distribution as they came upon the needy. The logic seems simple to me and I can buy into this because I hate not helping, but I hate even more feeling like I've been taken in by a professional panhandler.

This is something you could do as an individual, or you could get your scout troop, fraternity, sorority, church, synagogue, or temple involved in. Each bag costs between one and two dollars; if you buy in bulk the costs will go down. This allows you to be a wary Samaritan while simultaneously being a Good Samaritan. You can even get in some advertising for your cause (whatever your cause might be) by dropping information in the bag. Just as certainly as I believe there's a huge cadre of scammers out there, I also believe there are genuinely needy people out there you could help.

Cautious Strangers

At times a Good Samaritan's acts of kindness shocks people. I was pushing my cart through the Costco parking lot today so I could unload it in my truck when I spied a lady, at least 20 years my senior, working her way to the cart rack a hundred and fifty feet away. She was moving at an obviously struggling gait. When I drew alongside her, I asked if I could take her cart. Seeing that I had a full cart of my own she seemed puzzled by my offer. I then said, "I'll take it to the cart rack if you'll allow me too." At this point she broke into a smile and thanked me as she turned back to her car. This was my good deed for the day and I hope it brightened her day as well. A wary Samaritan understands trepidation at being approached by a stranger in a parking lot, but even today not everyone who approaches you in a parking lot means you ill or wants your money.

Weary In Well-Doing

Every once in a while, I have a day where it seems like the little bit of good I'm able to do is completely overwhelmed by the volume of need and level of evil I encounter in the world. I know the scriptures admonish us to "…not become weary in well doing." It even goes on to say we'll reap the benefit or reward of our good works if we are diligent and don't give up. For a wary Samaritan, some days it's a lot easier to be discouraged than it is to be diligent.

Become Engaged

I ventured through a neighborhood today where I spent two years living and working more than a decade ago. It was the backdrop of my daily life while completing my master's degree. It was and is predominantly African-American, with a smattering of Hispanics, and the occasional Anglo or Native American. There were notable changes in the area from when I first moved in. There were three new low-income apartment complexes and there was a new health clinic for the area's poor. I don't know how much, if any of that, I had a hand in, but I know how hard some of us in the community worked to bring in two supermarkets (i.e., FoodMaxx® and Albertson's®), affordable day care, a food pantry for the poor, and health care for an area of nearly 100 square blocks. This was an effort by individuals, churches, business, and local government. There is zero danger you will ever become a wary Samaritan while sitting around the house in your gated community.

We All Need A Good Samaritan Sometime

I barely managed to squeeze into a parking space at one of those Habitat For Humanity Re-Stores today in Irwindale, CA because the space ahead of me where I was originally destined was suddenly cut-off by a man who whipped around me and backed in. This left me fully in the back space, in a full-size pickup truck, and at a severe angle. I decided to go ahead and go inside and watch the space so I could exit as soon as the Backer left. I didn't want to impede anyone else and the guy parked next to me looked like he was seriously working and not just looking, as I was.

Eventually I needed to leave and Mr. Backer hadn't bought anything, he didn't have a basket, and seemed to just be killing time. I saw that Mr. Serious Work Guy was preparing to leave, so I figured I better go out and get my truck out of his way. When I approached him and explained why I was parked at an 80-degree angle, he said, "No problem." When I got in my truck, Mr. Backer had decided to leave and I figured I'd just pull ahead and get on the road. Mr. Serious Work Guy had other ideas and wanted to guide me out.

At first I thought about waving him off and then I recalled what a good attitude he had (i.e., "No problem") and so I figured I was gonna let him do his Good Samaritan thing. Letting him guide me back and then out probably took a lot longer than if I'd just pressed ahead, ignored him altogether, and drove on my way. After all, I'd never likely see him again. Instead, I al lowed him to do something I hate, allowing someone else to be in charge of my life. He eventually got me out of the lot and on my way. I waved to him as I headed east toward the 210 Freeway.

So what is the wary Samaritan point to be learned here? The point is you can't always be in the driver's seat in life. Sometimes it's a case where you've no choice but to be the recipient; occasionally it's because you choose to let someone else take charge. It doesn't hurt you once in a while to allow other people live out their Good Samaritan inclinations on you. You don't always have to be the hero in every situation. So lighten up and if people try to help you or bless you in some way, even if it's not your first inclination, let them! While you're considering the matter, you might consider how many times in your life other people allowed you help them.

The Times They Are A Changin'

It doesn't normally occur to my way of thinking someone who intervenes in a violent situation, and in saving an innocent's life is forced to end another life, could be regarded as a Good Samaritan. I do recognize Good Samaritans come in all shapes and sizes and rise up in all sorts of real-life situations. Now understand I'm not a pacifist and never have been. I recognize peoples' right to self-defense and to the defense of others. If I didn't fully understand how this worked before, law school helped me get a clear picture of the legalities involved. That's correct Virginia; people have a right in the United States to protect their own lives and the lives of others. I know it's not politically correct, but for some reason folks have long felt like they should be able to live out their lives unmolested.

I'm not suggesting we all go out and become vigilantes. I'm suggesting it takes a special kind of courage to come out of our safety and anonymity and stand up for an innocent life, the life of our loved ones, or the lives of total strangers. As violent and unpredictable as our world has become, rather than being an intermittent event, we may come to see this form of Good Samaritanism on the rise out of sheer necessity. During the 14 years I was a pastor I learned there are moments when the only thing which will stop people bent on doing evil is to make it clear you'll resist their force with equal and/or greater force. Being a wary Samaritan doesn't mean being an uninvolved Samaritan! Being a wary Samaritan involves remaining engaged in life at all its levels when looking the other way would be far easier.

Lacking Compassion

In recent years I've regularly interacted with a young man who shows not the least inclination to go out of his way to help anybody else or show even a small amount of compassion to others he sees to have a need. I think of myself as a wary Samaritan, but never as an anti-Samaritan, or Narcissist. I've now observed this young man's behavior over a two-year period and at first I hoped I was just not seeing the more compassionate side of him. More recently I see this is the real him, not an aberration. This is a loss he does not realize for him and others like him. The worst part is I see it more and more among this young man's generation.

I'm not certain if it's something unique to today's 20-year olds, or just a few who have popped out to me as I go about my daily business. The idea we each are the center of our own little universe is alien to me and I believe it's alien to most of my generation. I came from a time which embraced the concept that "No man is an island." We were indoctrinated with ideas of love, compassion, peace, and altruism. But what I'm encountering now are many teens and young adults who seem solely self-focused. If this trend continues into future stages of their adulthood, both their lives and the world will be a darker and much less compassionate place.

Narcissism, a growing problem in this age, offers one explanation for the aforementioned behaviors. I'm of the opinion narcissism has reached epidemic levels. I see a generation of over-indulgent helicopter parents and grandparents as partial sources of the problem. On my way through a 40-year career I used to periodically encounter men and women who were narcissists. As I visit with businesses, churches, and government agencies today I find it's no longer the periodic encounter and I can usually count on meeting one or more in any sizeable organization. This is a sad problem for our society as I believe extreme levels of narcissism can and should be regarded as a form of mental illness. Sadly, if a narcissist is in a high enough position, when the narcissist finally implodes the organization can go with them.

Good Samaritanism is in danger of extinction in every generation. It seems to be an even greater possibility in an age of increasing self-absorption evidenced by rampant narcissism. My hope for all wary Samaritans is that we can have a different impact on our own children and grandchildren. It's okay they see we are wary; but only so long as they also see we cautiously overcome our wariness in order to be able to live out our Christian faith before the world. This is not now, nor has it ever been, an easy task. You and I should encourage our offspring to live an introspective life. Our goal should be they come out of this introspection with a rounded view of their actual place in the universe and take up the mantle of Good Samaritanism.

Weighing My Day

Almost every day, as I come to the end of the day, I question myself about what I've contributed today to bettering human existence, which surpasses what I've taken or made worse today from this existence. Some days a wary Samaritan must judge he's taken more, sometimes even far more, than he's given back. Other days, you finish the day with a sense you're positively contributing to the world around you. Whoever you are, wherever you are, I challenge you to put more into this life every day than you take from it.

Self-Absorbed

I wrote about self-absorption elsewhere in this book and it got me wondering how many wary Samaritans it takes to make up for the one person who seems to pass through life in a completely self-absorbed state. You meet them on the highway, at the market, in politics, and even at your house of faith. They operate from the position all of life revolves around them. As a consequence, they cut you off in traffic, they push ahead of you in the checkout line, they press political agendas wholly to their benefit, and they always seem to have four cents worth to say at church when everybody else only gets to put in their two cents worth. Some days it seems like the self-absorbed crowd is winning. This is why it's more important than ever you and I are out there assisting a wounded world. Don't become bitter because of the self-absorbed. Don't strike out at them. Instead, pray God will open their eyes to the larger issues at hand, issues which don't focus on them at all.

Doing Well By Doing Good

Today I was reminded how doing a good deed improves my own outlook and mental health. I immediately recalled learning this in a psychology class as an undergrad, but in the hustle and bustle of the ensuing years it had drifted from consciousness. What this means for me and you is being a Good Samaritan is a two-way street. Yes, it does help improve the lives of those we reach out too. However, it also improves our own lives while we're at it.

It's A Big Deal To The Recipient
When I reflect on acts of kindness I've seen performed by countless Good Samaritans, I've observed most of those actions took one minute or less. Of course I've seen these acts take ten minutes, an hour, a week, and perhaps even a lifetime, but most are of relatively short duration. This seems all the more reason to engage in Good Deeds since they cost us so little in the way of time and yet can mean so much to the recipient. The cost benefit ratio here is extremely positive.

Good Deeds Are Not Always Obvious
Some days being a Good Samaritan only requires buying a candy bar you don't really want. It happens when a grade-schooler comes to your door raising money for her elementary school band. Many wary Samaritans have a crisper full of *World Famous Chocolate* bars or other similar treats they don't eat and didn't really want. You can always pass them out at Halloween.

Policeman Good Samaritan
This wary Samaritan's hat is off to the young policeman who made recent national news. This occurred when he was called out to conduct a health and welfare check on a family with six children. Upon arrival he discovered they were without food. He then used his own money to provide food for them immediately.

Now certainly there'd be public resources available to feed these kids in time. But instead of being forced to wait hungry for the public resources to make their way through the requisite red tape, this Good Samaritan reached into his own pocket to make a difference at the immediate point of need.

Broadcasting False Signals Of Benevolence

This wary Samaritan has served on many charitable boards over the years and I continue to belong to clubs, associations, and faith-based groups which seek to perform good deeds of all sorts. I was talking with an old friend today who's found himself similarly situated over the years in his own efforts to make a difference in the world. One of the things we both found simultaneously annoying and amusing is how many people join such organizations, are minimally active, are minimal donors, but want to have maximum input and to be seen by others as major players in the group's accomplishments. Wouldn't it be better to be the real deal instead of a poser? Of course there's a cost involved in being the real deal.

Many of us have seen people insist they be placed on committees charged with distribution of some fund or other, a fund the entire group raises. Simultaneously I've been in a position to know not only did these same people not donate to the fund, they barely involve themselves enough financially to remain on the membership roles. Imagine my shock recently upon hearing one such freebooter talking to a group of donors about how glad he and his wife were to be able to contribute to the effort "so generously in recent years." With regard to being a donor, follow Teddy Roosevelt's advice… "Walk softly and carry a big stick." The wary Samaritan interpretation of this line is "Donate generously but don't broadcast it."

I've chaired fundraising efforts where social media was involved. I find social media to be a mixed blessing. Here people can easily disseminate information about an opportunity to take part in a good deed and can quickly and cheaply get out the word to thousands. Where I've been dumbfounded has been in instances where people went on social media and talked about how they support the effort, encouraged others to give, and promised they'd give generously. People are duly impressed. However, as chair when it's been my job to follow up on the claimed promise, many of these same folks either accuse me of misinterpreting their social media comments or tell me they won't donate. Our social media friends are left believing them to be generous donors while in fact the rest of us are left to pick up the slack.

Shared Missions

Every once in a while, a wary Samaritan has to sit down and reassess his or her efforts in light of the concept of return on investment. I encourage each of you to take some time yearly and consider the clubs, schools, or faith-based groups you work with and see if your path and their path is still the same. If the paths begin to diverge, you probably need to figure out whether you're off your path, they're off their path, or it's time both your paths parted. There's an old scripture from the Book of Amos which comes to mind here, "Can two walk together, except they be agreed." These are good words to ponder as you reflect on shared missions from the past and those you may consider taking on in the future.

Cautious Good Samaritan

This wary Samaritan and his much less wary wife were coming out of In-n-Out Burger tonight and at the stop light there was a young fellow standing there holding a sign which said he was hungry and homeless and would work for food. Ignore for the moment it was already getting dark and unless you needed a night watchman, the latter offer was meaningless.

The wife looked at him and then at me and said, "Should we help him?" I was within three feet of him on my side of the car and looked him over from head to foot before responding. "He's wearing a new two hundred fifty-dollar pair of tennis shoes and the ones I own cost me $30 from the closeout rack at Big-5®." I realized the rustle I was hearing was the sound of my wife putting money back in her purse.

It's appropriate here to mention my wife is a naturalized American Citizen and has been in this country going on two decades. She spent time living under the Communists after the war. Her family was on the losing side of that war and she and others were incarcerated at various times under the Communists. Later she spent six and half years living in an internment camp in Malaysia. As a result of her love of this country, her sympathies are higher for Americans and her wariness of American con artists/beggars is lower than mine.

Please kind hearted people, look at who you're about to give money to before you toss away those Washingtons, Lincolns, and Hamiltons. Hang onto them until you amass a Jackson, a Grant, or a Franklin and find some truly needy person or needy family to share it with. If a hungry and homeless person keeps better hours, is cleaner, and better dressed than you are, why not ask them to help you out instead.

A Messed Up And Deadly World

A friend of mine shared with me the other day about trying to help a family who was struggling with a host of problems (e.g., unemployment, addictions, spousal abuse, child-rearing issues, etc.). The more he tried to help, the further he got pulled into their family drama. It finally came down to the point where police, social services, and the child welfare folks were all involved.

At this point my friend was able to pull away, but only because everyone else involved was going to be detained by one or more of the aforementioned authorities. I remind you throughout my speaking and writing to be cautious, tread softly, and avoid putting your life at risk. It's a needy world, but it's also a messed up and deadly world if you run afoul of the wrong people. Take care out there!

Road Hazard

I stopped this morning at a stop sign and once I made it around the corner I parked and walked back to the intersection. I looked both ways and then walked out into the street. I picked up a three-inch long deck screw lying there, which I'd carefully avoided running over. I'm wary about many things. In this case I was able to address two things I care about at the same time. First, I was able to avoid getting a screw in one of my truck tires. Second, I was able to remove the screw from the roadway and possibly save another driver from a worse fate than I'd experienced.

If you're like me you've had all the flat or destroyed tires you want. By taking three or four minutes of my time I may have spared you a flat tire or even an automobile accident. So the next time you see an object lying in the roadway, if you can safely do so, please take a minute, pick it up, and dispose of it properly. If it's too big or the roadway is too dangerous, you can let your highway department or highway patrol know and they can take care of it. They'd much rather clean up a road hazard than a car wreck or a fatality.

Christmas Is Coming And Con Artists Will Soon Upon Us

You know just as sure as the weather begins to cool, the holidays are just a few weeks away. This wary Samaritan used to be one of those people who just dreaded the holidays and experienced the holiday blues most years. I've worked hard to overcome those feelings and for the most part truly enjoy the holidays as I've grown older. I think giving helps my holiday blues and elevates my own mood.

One aspect of the holidays I've never learned to appreciate are the high level of beggars, con artists, and hucksters suddenly going into holiday gear. I frequent a shopping center where the same young woman has been hungry and homeless for each of the past five holiday seasons. She works her way back and forth across the parking lot for about three hours a day, but only Monday through Friday.

My approach to the holiday season now and to each of these Grinch-like pitfalls is to work harder than ever to find people who are actually in genuine need. This means people not just wanting extra cash, extra booze, or extra drugs for the holiday season. When you find a truly needy person or persons, then open your heart fully and share the best you have to offer. May your every Christmas be joyous.

Maybe You Should Consider A Divorce

We should all make a point of getting to know the charities we donate to. We should cease to be taken in by the well-manicured public image; many of them pay Madison Avenue advertising firms to create and sustain these images. The largest amounts of money and other tangible resources given by my wife and me at year's end are given to non-profit organizations devoted to some form of charitable work.

What we've learned over the years is not all charities are created equal, some get better with time, and some change for the worse over time. Some are scrupulous with our donations while others treat donations like a personal piggy bank. Some have a cadre of hard-working poorly paid employees while others are at the other end of the spectrum with overpaid and underperforming employees.

I've entirely dropped support for some groups I used to be generous with, either because their goals and mine were no longer the same, or because I began to notice they didn't seem to be the good stewards of our money as they'd once been. Opulent offices and expensive fundraising campaigns were eating a growing share of the annual funds. I ran two sizeable non-profits; I recognize troubling signs most people don't.

As we head toward the Christmas season, year's end, and the giving to avoid income taxes season, you're going to be receiving more solicitations plucking at your heart strings in an attempt to get you to open your checkbook. It's up to you and me to check out these professional fundraisers to see if they're legitimate and full of good works or just well-oiled and adept at soliciting and spending your money.

I use reports from groups like Charity Navigator to help me understand a little bit more about organizations which are not headquartered in my local area. For years now they've guided me away from some questionable charities and led me to charities with a good track record all around. I value a low overhead organization where most of the money is going to the cause it's raised for and not on fundraising or extravagant executive salaries.

Some of us see our money as belonging to God, some don't. In either case your money is your responsibility. If you're a wary

Samaritan, you really care about the amount of good each dollar you donate accomplishes and not just feeling relieved you've donated to something. Most Good Samaritans are not wealthy people and truly want their donations to help the needy. Finally, there are some groups you've supported in the past where it may be time to consider a trial separation or even a divorce.

Who Dropped The Ball

Elsewhere in this book and in speaking I've shared with you about stopping to pick up a screw which was in the roadway in an effort to spare someone else a flat tire. I encouraged everybody to consider taking on some of this kind of behavior. Apparently one of you didn't listen well or I should have written this book sooner; today I noticed a bright shiny screw in my right rear truck tire. I thought it might not be long enough to have penetrated and headed for the tire shop to have it assessed. I was praying I'd make it without going flat and simultaneously fearing it was leaking at a breakneck pace.

When I arrived at the tire dealership, the manager assured me it was leaking and sprayed some soapy water on the screw to prove his point. The sight and sound of the bubbles was blinding and deafening to my core. I was crushed one of you hadn't caught it. Come on people! I can't do this alone and there are lots of careless folks out there who drop tire eating objects every day. Be on the lookout! It will be a twofer, you get points for being a Good Samaritan and you keep cantankerous old people like me out of tire repair shops.

CHAPTER 9

Anna "Neeley" Rogers

If each one of us reflected on the good deeds which have been done for us in life, we'd realize less is often more. Seemingly small and insignificant acts of kindness toward me are still firmly in my memory a half-century later. Small kindnesses in fact make a huge difference in each of our lives. A wary Samaritan should consider this truth often and not behave as if one must go through life making grand gestures in order to impact the lives of others. Seemingly insignificant items such as a cup of water, a kind word, or a piece of wise advice given at a critical moment can change a person's universe for the better.

As I'm writing this my father's sister "Ann" recently passed away, she was 94. She was always the most kind-hearted and considerate of my father's sisters. She'd been burned horribly as a child and spent major parts of her younger years in a Catholic hospital being treated, taught, and raised by nuns and nurses. Once she was grown, she spent the rest of her life working as a school teacher in a Catholic school and as a professional nurse. When I was a boy I was terribly nervous and stuttered constantly. In visiting our home she noticed this and also noticed I bit my nails until they bled. On a visit when I was about 8 years old, she called me to her side and handed me a nail clipper. I didn't have a nail clipper; I didn't need a nail clipper because I didn't have any nails.

"Farrell", she said. "I've noticed you chew on your nails all the time. Son, this is because you're anxious, just as my father was anxious and your Daddy is anxious. You bite your nails because they're ragged and the raggedness causes you to constantly try to smooth them out." She opened the nail clipper and inside was a small steel nail file. "I'm going to file each of your nails as best as I can with them already so short. But from now on when your nails make you anxious you're going to pull out this set of clippers and file your nails until they're smooth." She looked at me for effect and asked, "Do you understand?"

Now up to this point in my life I'd never considered you could do anything with a problem beyond constantly picking at it. Suddenly, here was my aunt telling me I could take charge of something which drove me crazy and resolve it. It was a revelation of a magnitude so immense I can't properly express it here. This understanding would soon help me when Mildred Collins worked to help me overcome stuttering. As a consequence, throughout the rest of my life I've taken the position I can effect positive change which will make my life better. All of this from a $1 nail clipper and a file. I still carry nail clippers and files with me each day and keep them in all my briefcases, desks, and vehicles.

I haven't bitten my nails in over 50 years. It seems funny in retrospect such a small act of kindness should make such a major difference in my life. You see, small things can empower people in larger ways than we imagine. If you're the kind of wary Samaritan who searches for the grand gesture, you might be more effective at times by lowering your sites. The tools which I've used to build my personal life and professional career were often given to me as small acts of kindness by caring people who already possessed those tools. Teaching a small boy how to file his nails doesn't seem so significant does it? Yet I couldn't be the man I am today without what my Aunt Ann shared all those years ago.

Good Deeds Are More Important Now Than Ever

A wary Samaritan will readily observe there's no shortage of bad news in the world; just reading the local paper daily drives this truth home. I live near a large city where murders, robberies, rapes, assaults, and tragic deaths are part of the daily news.

In recent years I've seen people lose their jobs, homes, marriages, and in more than one instance, their minds. All across the nation the tough economic times have melted into the national psyche and become the backdrop of our everyday lives.

This is why the work of Good Samaritans is more important now than ever. Times where the tides of good are lowest are the time doers of good deeds are more needed than ever. As hard as it seems, we need to increase our efforts and not decrease them.

I suggest you at least consider doing as I do, every time I see an evil deed or circumstance it motivates me to try harder than ever to do good. Of course you can cynically argue one person alone can't turn the tide for the whole country, and you'd often be correct in such estimation.

However, I also know from personal experience and those of other wary Samaritan friends how one person can make a true difference in the lives of one other person, one family, or even a whole community. You and I need to be such persons.

Power In Smiles And Kind Words
There are times where something as simple as offering a smile or a kind word can be uplifting for both parties. In the life of a wary Samaritan there've been moments when a smile or a kind word from another person lifted my spirits and made an otherwise hard day easier to bear.

The point here once again is good deeds don't always have to be enormous efforts or big gestures. In a steadily coarsening society, simply being polite and well-mannered in social encounters goes a long way toward making peoples' day. Try it today and see if it doesn't lift your own spirits as well.

We All Need Beautiful Music
I don't know how you feel about music, but for me music can be one of the most wonderful experiences in life; I listen to music every day. I like several types of music and have quite eclectic tastes. For those of you who are musicians, I'm not. So let me say thank you for sharing the gift you have with the rest of us.

Yesterday I listened on YouTube® to a collection of street musicians in various locales around the world playing "Stand By Me." Their effort is called *Playing For Change*. Some of them were adequate, some were brilliant, and some were clearly working out mental demons through their music. It was still a beautiful experience for me to hear and see them play.

This wary Samaritan encourages you to support music wherever you find it. My family raises money in support of music and other fine arts in public schools in memory of my son Ryan. The world needs beautiful music and so much of it begins in the hearts and minds of school children. Please consider doing something similar in support of music the next time you encounter musicians, young or old, who could use your support.

A Good Samaritan's Integrity

Regardless of how much you want to make the world a better place, there'll always be people who misunderstand your intent and malign whatever effort it is you make. There's a great deal to be said in the positive about walking in your own integrity. Go ahead and let others be as they will, but keep your own integrity.

Wary Samaritans discover on occasion that all which empowers them to go on in their journey comes from knowing their heart was right and their efforts true. As much as we might wish it, none of us can truly force other people to believe what we believe or to take our word for the motives behind our actions. It's usually fruitless to try.

We can take comfort in knowing in the future all the hidden things will be revealed and the actual intents of our hearts will be known. Until this moment arrives, you can expect at times your best efforts will be denigrated and the purity of your motives repeatedly called into question.

This state of affairs says more about the darkened nature of men's hearts than it says about anything pertaining to you.

Take A Break

A wary Samaritan can often find it wearying to be constantly preferring others before herself, even when the scriptures she reads admonish her to exhibit this kind of behavior. Don't think you're the only one who at times feels a little put out at always trying to be the giving one, the kind one, the concerned one, or the helping one. Be cautious here and remind yourself once every five or six days to set a pace you can live with and not get burned out. There's a lot of garbage out there these days, perhaps more so than ever before.

This garbage-atmosphere means whatever route you take to avoid or defuse your pent up frustrations, be sure to go there as often as it takes to keep you sane and still scouring the ditch for the next victim. I rejoice when I hear a report of people doing good deeds. I encourage you to fill your mind with positive stories about the good deeds all around us. I know the media doesn't always promote these stories because the drama of violence, avarice, and destruction sells. Despite all this salability, negative information of this sort troubles our minds and loads down our hearts.

I know how hard it is to feel like you always need to be reaching out to others who have less than you have. I also know at times Jesus had to take a break, whether by going away to pray, or by actually physically leaving the site of a particularly taxing portion of his earthly works. On those occasions he often even sent his closest associates away. This reminds you and me at certain moments, even those we love and count as dear to our own lives can wear us down.

Here's some homespun wisdom I've heard. "It's better we come apart from others, in order to avoid coming apart ourselves."

Help Is On The Way

There was a sad story this week in the news about a man who was struck by a hit and run driver and no one would stop to help him. Older members of this reading audience will remember the Kitty Genovese case of many decades back where a young woman was stabbed to death and despite many people admitting they heard her pleas for help, no one initially went to her aid. Each wary Samaritan sees more and more of this growing phenomenon of what social psychologists call *Diffusion of Responsibility* and most of us don't like what we see.

We thought this was bad back in the 1960s and 1970s, but the problem has grown larger and worse instead of getting smaller and better. If anything, I suspect we're far more separated from our fellow human beings than we were 40 or 50 years ago, if for no other reason than our electronic shields, shields which come in the form of computers, smart phones, and iPads®. This is not a healthy trend for a society. Societies form so humans can work together to their mutual benefit. When everyone turns back to thinking only about themselves, we've returned to the law of the jungle and incivility follows.

I suppose some who drove past this hit and run victim were hurrying to something important, others were likely afraid to get involved, and others still probably said to themselves, "It's not my problem." As it was, the man was able to help himself and fortunately he survived. The English Common Law taught us unless we have some sort of special duty to a victim, we have no legal obligation to stop and assist in these matters. However, a Good Samaritan's heart should reflect a different kind of law. Government thinks so too and developed the so-called Good Samaritan Laws to make it easier to help without getting sued for your efforts.

In this book you'll notice the subtle message that not everyone is able to be of help in every situation. Despite this effort at subtlety, I hope you'll also gain the sense everyone is able to help in some situations. Be on the lookout for those places you can help, and if nothing more you can dial 911 if you see an accident such as this one, but don't feel you can or should stop to help. You'll at least have done your part to assure some kind of help is on the way to the fellow at the side of the road. Every one of us has those times in his or her life where we desperately need a Good Samaritan. Think about one of those times when you experienced this kind of the next time you want to just drive on by.

Brighten Someone's Day

My middle daughter Melody, worked as a Nanny for several years. One day as she was trying to watch over the two small children in her charge, she was also trying to fold up a double stroller and place it in her vehicle. She said a man came up and asked if he could help her. When she consented he folded up the stroller and placed it in the trunk of her car. Of course a wary Samaritan's first instinct was concern this was some sort of scam; it wasn't.

She said this was the first time in all the years she's been a Nanny, and the first time in hundreds of foldings and unfoldings of a stroller, anyone has ever offered her help. She mentioned how much this encouraged her about people's kindness and brightened her day. I tell you throughout this book, in my speaking, and in my other writing it doesn't take enormous efforts or tons of money to make the world a better place. This was an excellent example of this principle.

In Some Way Inconvenient

Periodically I go back to the seminal text in the scripture of the Good Samaritan. I do so to remind this wary Samaritan of the exemplar. It struck me again as I meditated on his example today how the whole encounter with the man on the roadside was inconvenient. There are certainly other lessons to be learned from what transpired that day, but the over-riding thing I see time and time again is breaking up his trip, his day, and his life was just a total inconvenience. Yet there is no record of him complaining, worrying about the time, or trepidatiously counting the shekels in his bag, much less any hint he was put out or put off.

Don't take me wrong here, I think about this man a lot and at times I think perhaps he was just one of those characters who go through their entire lives nonplussed. Then again I ask myself how likely this scenario is. I come back to the reality this detour in his life had to have been in some way inconvenient for him. It cost him time, money, emotion, physical effort, miles on his journey, a late arrival at his next stop, maybe even an angry spouse who expected him a day earlier and with more money in his pockets. Of course, this is the lesson isn't it? In one way or another it's always inconvenient to perform Good Works.

Secret Good Samaritan

I watched a news report yesterday detailing how more and more people have taken the message of *Pay It Forward* to heart and become secret doers of good deeds. I found this to be some of the most heartening news I received this week. Now be wary, but get out there and perform good works this week. You can do them openly if the situation calls for it or you can do them in secret. Either way you do them it will bless someone else and you.

Words Of Encouragement

An encouraging word can often mean as much to people in time of distress as being pulled from a misadventure in a roadside ditch. Wary Samaritans are routinely surprised by how simple words of encouragement can lift the spirits and reinvigorate the will of those they're spoken to. So the next time you're thinking your ability to be a Good Samaritan is limited due to your age, income, or intellectual abilities, remember there's still considerable power to do good with your words.

Check Before You Hit "Send"

I received an email from a dear friend as I was writing this book. Attached was a purported expose' on all the bad charities one should not donate too and all the good charities one should donate too when contemplating one's year-end tax implications. There was only one problem with this well-intentioned email; the information was incorrect almost to the point of being an outright lie. How do I know this? I know this because for the past five years I've received this same email each year and each year I go back to www.snopes.com to see if anything has changed.

Snopes continues to rate it as mostly untrue. The sad part is this email defames some good and highly efficient charities, and then champions some charities with efficiency ratings as low as 35%. Please, please, please would-be wary Samaritans, check out information before you blast-mail it to all your contacts and help perpetuate a series of lies or misinformation. Snopes says this one has been making the rounds for at least the last eight year-ends. As I write this it's 2015. This means it's a lie going back to 2007. Be a wary Samaritan, not a bearer of false witness.

Sharing You

This wary Samaritan spent a lot of years working with my hands and developing a wide range of technical skills, several of which I became certified, registered, or licensed for. One of the ways I've tried to live out my Good Samaritan leanings is to offer advice when I encounter people in hardware stores or other similar venues who are DIYers trying to save a few bucks in these tough times. You have to know by now almost none of the big box stores, and very few of the mom and pop stores, can afford to hire anyone who knows much about plumbing, electric, carpentry, gardening, or any one of a dozen other skilled trades.

As a result, a trained eye shopping in one of these venues will occasionally see a potentially dangerous or expensive mistake about to be made. I'm not suggesting you put your professional license on the line or take bread out of your children's mouths, but it wouldn't kill you to be just a little bit helpful, providing the people will accept your help. I recently stopped a young man from converting the plug on his 12 volt DC vacuum cleaner to a 115 volt AC. He was launching a portable car wash service because he'd lost his job and figured all electric was the same. At first I could tell he didn't believe me, but after I showed him the rating on the plugs and explained the difference, he abandoned a bad plan.

Each of you has special gifts. Some of you have many special gifts. This is the way God made you. Most of us make our living with some or all of the gifts we possess. But just as it's a good thing to share our largess with those who don't have enough, it's a good thing to share your knowledge with people who don't have enough also. In hard times like so many are facing these days, there's a lot more opportunity to live out The Good Samaritan's

Creed like this than there is to be walking the highways looking for people who've been set upon by bandits. I admit I've had people become wary or annoyed, but the vast majority seem genuinely grateful someone cared.

No Small Kindnesses

Today I watched a young man freeing a jammed shopping basket from a mass of jammed shopping baskets at Home Depot®. He then turned and surrendered it to an elderly lady standing behind him. I offer here this small example once more of how much small kindnesses serve to make life better and brighter. In my estimation the young man couldn't help but feel better about himself and this would likely lift his self-esteem. The elderly lady was left with a sense of relief and gratitude and the knowledge there are a lot of good young people out there, even if it doesn't make the news. These actions and the resultant positive emotions they elicit ripple across our world to offset some of the uglier realities of our times.

Sharing Traffic Lanes

Don't you find it heartening when people will allow other people to go ahead of them in traffic? We all have to deal with heavy traffic so much on freeways and Interstates here in the West. Traffic congestion is a real and ongoing issue, which affects the quality of everyone's life.

This wary Samaritan has noticed over the years the two main causes of traffic jams on freeways is either a person who decides they'll speed to the very end of the multi-lane merging queue and force their way in, or the person who blocks people who are trying to merge steadily along the way.

Why not live out your Good Samaritanism by gracefully allowing others to merge? And if you're one of those people who drive 90 miles an hour all the way to the final merging point, why not grow up and share the highway? I shake my head at these moments of angry or selfish behavior because many of them are drivers with Christian messages on their bumper stickers.

Lowered Expectations

As any of you who follow my work or my writings knows, this wary Samaritan has a somewhat jaundiced view of your and my efforts to do good. It's not because our efforts aren't noble and well-intentioned, it's because too often you and I are the people who gets the soup spilled on us by the people who go through life spilling the soup. I hope for the best, but accept it might not go down this way.

My children heard me say frequently when they were young "No good deed goes unpunished." I also reminded them they should perform good deeds despite this warning. So on one hand I encourage you to reach out as best you can to a troubled and needy world, but on the other hand don't expect any ticker-tape parades in your honor for your efforts. Do expect things could go awry.

There seem to be at least as many stories out there about Good Samaritans injured or killed while trying to live out their values as there are stories about them being hailed as heroes and given the keys to the city. You'll keep doing good because God has placed this desire in your heart, not because you hope they'll throw a parade in your honor and name a grammar school after you.

If by some chance you should ever be honored for your good deeds, take it in stride and with the same level of equanimity you previously took the other thousand efforts you made which no one but you, the recipient, and God took notice of. It's okay to be slightly pessimistic if you can routinely overcome your own pessimism and take action when it's needed. Be most concerned about how your heavenly Father views your works.

Killing Me Isn't Part Of The Good Samaritan Paradigm

We're each reminded in the Bible to initially count the cost of any undertaking. Wary Samaritans everywhere should see this is as good advice, especially when living out your Good Samaritan side. The actor Clint Eastwood portrayed a character once who remarked famously, "A man's got to know his limitations." My perspective is you and I need to know our limitations; can we truly pay the total cost entailed. If we don't know our limitations, we may well endanger both ourselves and others we come to aid.

Some years back I witnessed a Good Samaritan rendering first aid to the victim of an automobile accident. She did so after shooing me and several other away people who had stopped to help, all the while assuring us she was an expert in first aid. The victim was clearly going into shock with a pale face, cold clammy skin, and shallow respiration. The first people to arrive had elevated the man's feet about a foot to force blood flow back to the brain. The first aid expert who ran everyone else off immediately lowered the feet and raised the man's head.

About that time, the Paramedics arrived and chased her away from the patient. As she was proudly telling them what she'd done to stop the other responders' mistreatment, one of the Paramedics said, "It's lucky we got here when we did. If you'd kept his head up much longer he would've gone into full-blown shock and died." She fell silent and moved toward the back of the circle of onlookers. What she'd done would've been good practice for treating heat stroke; it could've been deadly to someone going into shock.

God doesn't expect you to jump into every single tragic circumstance you encounter. Remembering pride is said to precede a fall, I'd remind each of us if we're not 100% sure of our limitations in moments like those I've just described, it might be better to ask if there's anyone in the crowd who knows more about what's going on than you or I do. I appreciate Good Samaritans, but only if they aid and comfort me; killing me is not part of the Good Samaritan paradigm.

Living In Garbage

A wary Samaritan looks around each day for good deeds because they're part of the positive flow in the world which energizes and encourages us. Most of the time they're small things and you have to condition yourself to spot them or they go completely unnoticed. The big event good deeds, when they do occur, are in your face and nearly impossible to ignore.

If you and I wish to live a happier and more tranquil existence as wary Samaritans, we have to work as hard to spot the good going on around us as we fight to filter out the evil and negative which seems to flood in from many sources. You're in charge of your thought life! You and you alone have the power to assure whether it's positive or negative. You can compel positive change in your life more than anyone else.

Consider the disparate voices which pull at you each day. The ones you turn up and tune in to will have the greatest impact. To diminish their impact, tune out their voice. To enhance their impact, tune up their voice. There are times you and I need to be very particular about the things we allow to enter our consciousness or we may find our consciousness has been trashed and we're living in garbage.

Sharing The Knowledge You Possess

I speak and write about how important it is to share learning; it's a theme I feel passionately about and repeat often. I don't believe we can underestimate the value of sharing what we've learned with other people. I know the human reaction is to dismiss our own learning as something surely everyone already knows. I encourage each of you to share what you've learned at every opportunity. Some of us will have more opportunity to share our learning than others, some of us will have formal venues in which to share, and others still will be teaching what they've learned in informal settings like fields, forests, factories, oceans, or warehouses. Places where people can share and people can learn are nearly limitless. Don't let it enter your mind all learning takes place in formal settings.

Shared knowledge is a powerful thing! Shared knowledge is a beautiful thing. It can transform a person or an entire society. It can elevate health, happiness, and spirituality. In fact, knowledge is feared more by tyrants than guns and bullets. If we share our money, money is soon gone. If we share our ideals of physical beauty, physical beauty soon fades! But if we share knowledge, even knowledge of the most seemingly mundane interpersonal truths, this knowledge will eventually flourish, bloom, and bear fruit generation after generation. The most ordinary and mind-numbing tricks associated with hard labor, and the time passers which make bearable a workday's grinding routine can be priceless to those who need them.

Make Someone's Day

My Friday was made brighter early this morning when a young woman brought her vehicle to a stop and waved me across a busy shopping center driveway where I'd already waited for what seemed an interminable period. I smiled my best smile at her and waved my best wave; she returned both. What a nice young woman and what a nice way to launch the last workday of the week.

Good Deeds Aren't Hypothetical

"Esta es tu madre?" I asked the four-year-old girl as I pointed toward the sign-holding woman standing next to her on the curb? She brightened and responded immediately, "Si! Mi madre." I handed the child a twenty-dollar bill, the mother never spoke but tearfully nodded her thanks at the money. I rolled up the window and drove out of the Walmart® parking lot. As a wary Samaritan I'd just done something I rarely do; turn my truck around and drive back to give money to someone begging. In this case the sign said it was for rent and in the winter of 2008, after the economic collapse, I could easily believe it.

I'm still asking myself years later what it was I saw which told me these three (Momma had a baby in her arms) standing there by the driveway were the real deal and not just a clever con; I'd seen many other similar scenes which failed to move me. It might've been the young girl's innocent glee at people handing her money in stark contrast with her young mother's expressionless face. But it might have been I saw something in her mother's eyes, which I'd seen in my own mother's eyes, back in those bad winters in the early 60s when farm work was scarce, rent was hard to come by, and hunger wasn't a hypothetical concept as winter and the Holiday Season set in.

Almost Overwhelming

We can so insulate ourselves from the world around us that we become deaf, mute, and blind to the needs of others. Even a wary Samaritan has to discipline herself to remain attuned to the needs of those around her when the times she lives in are overwhelming due to a world so filled with suffering. The knowledge of vast need can definitely be overwhelming. Sometimes out of pure self-defense we try to tune the level of awareness of need down. It's at these times we must force ourselves to turn toward the need, face it, and listen.

No Good Samaritan's Remorse Today

When a wary Samaritan goes out of their way to aid another person, they generally know the next day if they've done the right thing or if they were just overcome by the emotion of the moment. Today I feel great about my choice yesterday to aid another person and her family. I have no Good Samaritan's remorse, just a sense of peace about having done the right thing.

CHAPTER 10

Huong Thi Tran: "I Never Forget This Lesson"

I've shared before in this book, my other writings, and public speaking how my wife Huong Tran is Vietnamese by birth and came here many years after the war. Between the end of the war and her arrival in the United States she was busy trying twice to escape the Communists, spent three years in a form of forced labor as punishment for the first escape attempt, escaped on her second attempt, and then spent six and a half years in an internment camp in Malaysia before being allowed to enter this country. There she endured many of the horrors common to internment camps; events most of us have only seen on television. Despite these struggles, she's still a caring person and her heart goes out to people in need, especially to children. She loves kids, having none of her own, and her job in the internment camp was to cook for the orphaned children there.

Huong, known to her friends and family here in the United States as Kim or sometimes Mrs. Neeley, was eventually allowed to come here based on the sponsorship of an Uncle who'd escaped at the fall of Vietnam. It helped that our government recognized that the Communist government's treatment of her father and her oldest brother either directly or indirectly killed both of them after the war. She knew when her father died, but her brother was imprisoned for his service and the family didn't know he'd died while imprisoned until they were told one day some years later they could come retrieve his bones. Her Uncle Phuc was also imprisoned; two years for each year he served as an officer in the Army of the Republic of South Vietnam. He told me his military career had been three years long; his prison term, with attendant tortures was six.

Now I shared this with you as an insight into my wife's life and not to solicit sympathy for a scenario many war refugees have faced throughout time. Yesterday I was at her nail shop. Yes, I know a Vietnamese woman owning a nail shop is a cliché in these times, but she really did save enough over the years before I met her to buy her own nail shop. As this story unfolds, it was late in the day on a Sunday and she was planning to close shop early because the day had been brutally cold and business had been slow. I'd come by to have one of the manicurists try to clear up an ingrown toenail. While I was sitting there, a bedraggled old man could be seen making his way from trash can to trash can in the parking lot out front, digging I imagined for aluminum or plastic he could sell to recyclers.

About this time my wife disappeared into the back of the shop and I could hear her rummaging around. I thought nothing of it since she's always on the move when she's not working on a client. I was puzzled however when the old man I'd observed stopped at the door to the shop, but didn't come in. He stood there patiently as the minutes ticked by. I continued to wonder what was going on. Eventually I saw my wife coming out of the back of the shop with a plastic sack full of aluminum cans and plastic two-liter drink bottles. She brought them to the door and handed them out to the old man. I heard him thank her for her kindness and he resumed his journey from trash can to trash can.

This wary Samaritan was somewhat surprised because generally my wife is devoted to sending any extra money she can to her family in Vietnam and a couple of orphanages there she supports faithfully. Through her I've come to know how desperate the need there is among the general populace and especially the orphans. I even have to remind her to give money to the local Catholic Church she attends. So I couldn't help but question her on this seeming change of giving strategy on her part. Her answer was perfectly in character. She said, "I see he try to have a better life. He work to have a better life. I see him try every week. When I come here people help me because they see I try. I never forget this lesson." Let all Good Samaritans be just as quick to help those who are trying.

More Than Poppies

Wary Samaritans across the nation annually encounter Veterans of Foreign Wars Poppy sales in their communities. I tell them right off "I don't want your poppies. What I want to do is to donate some money (e.g., $5, $10, $20) to support you and the work you do." It's not anything against the poppies… I want them to get more donors.

So if you run across a VFW member selling poppies, either buy a poppy or donate some money. At one point in their lives these men and women were ready to lay it all on the line to protect me and you and uphold our Nation's values. This is a service we should never forget or take lightly.

At Home First

Once again this week I was reminded the first place we should practice Good Samaritanism is in our own homes and with our own families. Once we have this habit firmly established, touching the rest of the world will come to us much easier. I witnessed a tragedy unfold among a Christian family, a tragedy which would've likely never occurred if the parents had turned their hearts toward their own home years ago instead of directing all their energy toward others. I ponder often how awful it would be to come to the end of our lives and be able to look upon vast good we did for many others, only to look around and realize how little we did for the handful of people God placed in our direct care; our family.

Wary Doesn't Mean Despairing

I encourage you to do as I do and be on the lookout for people doing good works every day. This is as much about your own mental health maintenance as it is about good works. Some days it's much easier to spot good deeds than others. But if I look intently enough each day, I can always find at least one. I like to think of myself as a wary Samaritan and not a melancholy or despairing Samaritan. I can only accomplish this by acknowledging the good being done in the world around me. Conversely I find on any day where I fail to follow this practice, I'm struggling with despair by the end of the day. It's possible I'm not alone in these feelings and so I offer this antidote to you my reader. Look for the good and the beauty in the world around you. Put forth the often considerable effort it takes to do this, even when you feel like all your energy has been drained by the bad and the ugliness around you. It will make a difference in you, so you can make a difference in others.

Modern Day Acts of Kindness

This wary Samaritan had several acts of kindness directed toward him recently when someone hacked my email account and sent out the usual crude comments and photos associated with such hackings. It is of course embarrassing and annoying when people hack your email and do those kinds of things. The kind acts toward me mentioned here were those of friends calling, texting, or emailing to let me know it happened and assuring me they knew it wasn't my handiwork. This is not to say I've never seen a crude comment or questionable photo in my social media feeds, it's just to say I'd never forward something like that to anyone, much less my email list. I'm blessed my friends know me.

It Was No Big Deal

I watched a young wife push the wheelchair of her husband to the checkout line at the pharmacy the other day as I brought up my purchases and stepped into the line behind them. The man was a double amputee and from their chatter with the cashier I also learned he'd lost his legs in combat. At his wife's mention of Afghanistan, he sat up ramrod straight, he still wore the military haircut as if to illustrate the point. The cashier rang up the items and they came to $7.72. At first the young man handed her 6 crumpled one dollar bills, then found and handed her one more. He asked how much more he needed and was told, "Another 72 cents." When he said, "I'll have to leave the toothpaste." The cashier replied, "That's okay." She bagged all the items.

He thanked the cashier as he took the bag and his wife began to roll him away. As I stepped to the counter the cashier, a young woman of perhaps 20 years of age, reached into her pocked and pulled out a wrinkled dollar bill and placed it in the register. When this wary Samaritan laid down his items, she smiled and went about the task of ringing them up. Her face colored when I thanked her for what she'd done and she mumbled, "It was no big deal." Ah, but it was a big deal to me. It's always a big deal when I see one human being reaching out to another with a compassionate act. I'm not sure how many such acts this young man has seen to date, but I suspect he and his wife will need and receive many more in the years ahead.

Stealthy Good Samaritanism

Anytime you can do so safely it may be just as effective to allow someone who is struggling financially to perform some work for you as it is to hand them money without work. Here's my reasoning, in some parts of the country the winter time and holiday season is a down time for many industries and people are laid off until February or March or even April. Even with unemployment insurance, people still have a tight time of it under these circumstances. Why not hire them to perform some task for you?

Now I understand this can be dangerous, so I limit it to people I already know and have developed some sort of trust relationship with. In years past I've had men mow my lawns, trim my trees, and put out fertilizers for the winter rains to soak in. I've bought homemade food items, handmade clothing, and handicrafts from neighborhood ladies. I've even hired people to run errands for me I could've easily done myself. It never hurts to allow people to maintain their dignity. In fact, I'd recommend you always let people maintain their dignity where possible.

The point I'm making here is I find it preferable to allow people to maintain their personal dignity, rather than to force them to be reduced to receiving handouts or begging. Would you wish to be reduced to begging? I've given like this for years and I'm certain some in my neighborhood have come to count on this to help them get through the colder, wetter months when work in my agricultural area is extremely scarce. You know your world and you know your neighbors better than me; at least I hope you do.

Don't risk your life, your home, or your health to make this kind of effort, but when you can, if you safely can, it's okay to be a stealthy Good Samaritan. Good Samaritanism doesn't have to always be an "in your face" proposition. There's no reason you can't lend a helping hand to your fellow man without making a big show of it or even making it obvious what you're doing. This isn't a business of creating creditors and debtors, it's about expanding community and fostering brotherhood.

An Age Of False Prophets

I can't speak to the doctrinal positions of most religions. However I do feel somewhat capable of speaking to the doctrinal position of Christianity with regard to prophets. In looking at the issue closely, I'm reminded of how intolerant the Christian God is of prophets who prophesy and their prophesies do not come true. You see, while Spiritualists, Hindus, Muslims, and New Agers seem to gladly embrace any prophet or psychic with a fifty-one percent accuracy record, as better than average and therefore worth listening to, the Christian God declares anything less than one hundred percent as being unacceptable.

Now I'm not saying there can't be some element of human error in a prophet; say less than one percent simply due to human misunderstanding of what was heard or seen. A quick scan of the Old Testament would quickly dispel the flawless notion. But a lifetime of gross error in prediction is too much. So all of those out there Prophesying or claiming psychic insight about the return of the Nephilim, Wormwood barreling in from outer space any day, and the Messiah around every corner will really need to be on top of their game. Why? It's simple! There are going to be a lot of angry people hunting for them when it becomes apparent the end finally is coming.

People who took such seers seriously and deluded themselves into thinking fifty-one percent accuracy was really better than merely guessing, are not going to be amused. People, who paid for psychics to speak to the dead for them, or guide them in their life decisions, are going to be angry when the ruse is revealed. When the channels and channelers have been proved to be delusion, when people understand the full impact of a lifetime lived in error, then the phonies will need to flee for the caves of the mountains to save their lives. I suspect at such a time people driven crazy by the horror of the truth will seek their heads and not their advice.

What's this got to do with wary Samaritanism? It has to do with your credibility and how it impacts your ability to be effective as a Good Samaritan. If you're so busy espousing the ideas, dreams, and visions of the Prophet de jour, you distract people from why you're there and what your motivations are in the first place. If you've stepped onto the roadside to lend a helping hand, do not seize upon it as a time to proselytize, prophesy, or sell a copy of your latest self-help book. We live in an age of false prophets, cults of personality, and demigods; in such times a genuine Good Samaritan is water to a thirsty soul.

Facilitators Of Insight

Earlier today a friend of mine related how a simple gesture by a Good Samaritan had caused people to see a blind man in a whole new light, and to begin to reach out to him as they never before; their efforts were make his life better. As a wary Samaritan allow me I remind you that it's not always the cash you toss in the offering plate which has the greatest impact. Sometimes it's the simple act of helping others see real need in the truest light of day that has the most powerful and lasting impact. These insight facilitations hold the power to open wide the floodgates of human compassion.

Check Out That Charity

Many of the people out there raising funds for charities are not dedicated to the ideals of the charity, they're not unpaid volunteers, and they're in fact paid solicitors. There's nothing wrong with this in and of itself. But if you care about your charities, and you want the biggest bang for your buck, you need to sort out the wheat from the chaff in this area and donate accordingly. Organizations paying out 90% of their donations to paid solicitors or full time staff are only helping themselves.

There are an increasing number of means to determine what percentage of your donation actually gets into the hands of those in need; in my opinion the higher the amount staying for charitable works, the better. A truly wary Samaritan doesn't believe it's enough to say, "I gave." It's only enough in when you know you gave to a good work which gained the most bang for the buck, to the benefit of those you set out to aid in the first place. Stop being sloppy and lazy in your giving; check out those charities.

An Immigrant's Dream

Being able to help an immigrant become legally established in the country is an honor this wary Samaritan gladly embraces.

Today I helped one of my wife's employee's obtain a lease on her first apartment here in the United States. I also got her utilities activated and assisted her in moving into the new digs. I know, I know, some of you will say this is self-serving since your wife gets an employee who's now owned by the company store. This isn't our approach to life and owning people isn't part of our personal agenda.

As some of you are aware my wife Huong is Vietnamese and a naturalized United States citizen. I assure you the young woman I helped today had slept on the floor in a rented room at times and yet saved enough money after being here only 2 years to have a year's worth of rent in advance. If she chooses to walk, she certainly can. But for today she is and has been for many months now a valued employee and a new pursuer of The American Dream. Best wishes from a wary Samaritan, Minh!

My Scottish, Irish, and German ancestors began arriving here in 1703. My family is like most American families, it's a family of immigrants. When I think back to those who reached out to generations of Grandfathers Neeley, McCormick, Clopton, and Gober so they could set down roots here, it's a small thing for their descendant to offer a helping hand to another pursuing an identical dream. This is a great country, and regardless of what country you're in, treat immigrants the way you'd want to be treated.

Pick Your Own Charities
When I pass through checkout lines where the cashier is asking me to donate to their employer's chosen cause, if it also happens to be one of my chosen causes, I'm glad to join in and donate. But if I'm asked to donate to a cause which violates my conscience or

competes with a charity which I know does a better job; I refuse to be shamed into donating. Pick your own charities.

If the checker is nervy enough to ask why I won't donate, and I've had this happen more than once, I spell out for them in front of their other customers what I find objectionable about either the charity or the charity's approach to its mission. I don't use this approach as an opportunity to be rude; I see it as a teaching moment. Pick your own charities.

This is happening more and more in my online shopping; you know the ones where on-line retailers ask you to round up the total so the difference can be submitted to a charity. Many people do so without actually checking the options because they want to feel as if they've done a good thing. But when I began to follow the hyperlink to see what the 'selected' charities were, I often found they violated my conscience, ideals, or morals. Pick your own charities.

Know Your Trash, Know Your Treasures

I recently went to a great deal of trouble to salvage some computer power supplies because I knew they had resale value. My goal was to donate them to a local animal rescue group to which I donate items regularly. Imagine my surprise when they were refused. It seems while our local Bakersfield Association of Retarded Citizens (BARC) and other charitable groups will gladly accept these items, the animal rescue group doesn't. The volunteer wouldn't even allow me to lift the box out of my truck, as if I were unloading poisonous serpents.

It did no good to try to explain to the volunteer accepting my other donations how I'd personally checked each one out for performance integrity and they were all in excellent shape. My explanation made no difference to this lady; I understood she didn't make policy and let it go at that. Coincidentally, I was once COO for a medical non-profit which operated five small thrift stores. They raised a significant portion of our budget each year through the cast off donations of our generous supporters. The problem here is not with the volunteer, it's with the Board of Directors who set the policies. I also have to question what kind of information they're receiving from their CEO or COO.

Those Good Samaritans among you who serve on various non-profit boards owe it to your stakeholders to be on top of the donations aspect of the thrift shops you have open. That's not meant to sound trite. I know the market changes all the time and last year's trash is this year's treasure, and vice versa. In this case, I'll take the components to a couple of other local charities until I find one which understands they can pick up at least $90 in pure profit from the donation the other group refused. It's okay to be wary... but it's also important to stay on top of knowing the difference between trash and treasure when your good work depends on such knowledge.

CHAPTER 11

Alton 'Tony' Engel

I don't know about you, but some of the most transformative events which have come about in my life were the result of people reaching out to me in a positive way when I was young. Often I reflect on people who are long deceased, who for no discernible reason encouraged me, showed me a kindness, or offered me direction. Sometimes it was just a word or two of support. In other instances, it was a relationship which lasted for decades. I attended a memorial service this past weekend for one such man. It shouldn't have surprised me that there were at least six hundred people in attendance. It seemed each of them had somehow been touched by his personal brand of wary Samaritanism over his ninety-three years on Earth.

I like to think when people behave this way it's because of a similar loving act or acts which came their way when they were young and made their life better. It doesn't hurt to be trying to pass along or payback random acts of kindness you've received. In fact, it's one of those happenstances which makes life just a little more tolerable. In the case of the aforementioned gentleman, he was a widely celebrated professional in his area of expertise. Yet when I came to him as a total neophyte, he was warm and friendly and went out of his way to teach me some of the tricks of the trade. His mentoring me along the way made a professional and financial difference in my life over the thirty-six years I was blessed to know him.

Thank you Tony... RIP

Some Gave All

As I'm writing this it's Veteran's Day 2015 here in The United States and in our small town we place American flags in front of each business in the morning and remove them at the end of the day. In the bigger nearby city, there is a parade filled with men and women in uniform, as well as marching bands and equestrian groups. The size of the crowd waxes and wanes from year to year, depending on how popular or unpopular the nation's latest war is on the home front. Sometimes war is so unpopular there's no parade at all. Some years the parade is huge and effusive.

Almost twenty years back now this wary Samaritan witnessed a young boy of perhaps six or seven years or age, salute each float or vehicle of Veterans which passed his spot along the parade route. It seemed to invigorate the Veterans and it certainly animated the child. Being nosey by nature I eased toward where he and the young woman I took to be his mother, and what seemed to be an older sister, were standing along the curb. I wondered what had inspired this child to these efforts and reasoned others nearby would interrogate the mother for an answer. I wanted to be close enough hear it. Sure enough, near the end of the parade, she shared the details.

"He knows his Papa was a soldier who served in Vietnam. He was killed during his second tour of duty in 1965 near a place called An Loc, Binh Long province when it was overrun by battalions of North Vietnamese Regulars. My husband never knew his father, but we're career army now and my husband's a peacekeeper in Bosnia. My husband was conceived before his Dad left on his second tour of duty, and his Dad died when my mother-in-law was seven months along." All of us in the nearby crowd were silenced by her words, and the little boy went on saluting as before, unaware of the weight of his mother's words. It was an image I've never been able to shake through the ensuing years.

I think often of the smiles on the old Veteran's faces that Veteran's day and the smile on the face of the saluting little boy. I have to believe seeing this child dutifully saluting heartened those old Veterans... and somewhere there was a proud Papa returning his salute.

Keep Both Eyes Open

One only has to look at the newspapers, television, or Internet to understand how dangerous it can be in these times to reach out in kindness to another human being. I'm thinking specifically of the young math teacher who was known to be a caring and giving person. She was raped and murdered by a student she'd agreed to meet after regular class hours, in order to help with his math. We now know this was simply his pretext to lure her to her death. Most wary Samaritans are old enough they're not likely to change their ways. But for you fledgling Good Samaritans who may happen upon this book, please continue to love and give with all your heart, but keep both eyes open.

Identify Your Villains And Move On

As a wary Samaritan I do my best to reach out to any person who sincerely seems to be seeking to better themselves, their family, or their community. In a public meeting two years back I listened incredulously as someone I'd reached out to for over two years, repeatedly slandered me. When I challenged this slander, he refused to name a source or sources, and then refused to respond any further. In time it was revealed he'd secretly allied himself with political enemies of mine on promises they'd help further his career. They didn't follow through and he eventually lost his career altogether.

Despite this I continue to reach out to people in need, I'll not allow a single despicable person, or group of despicable people to rob me of the joy of performing good deeds. If you must have the assurance everyone you reach out to in good works will in turn be good and friendly toward you, you should cease your good works now! This kind of reciprocity has not been the case historically for Good Samaritans and it will not be the case in any foreseeable future. I think of Shakespeare and his use of the word villain with regard to those who betray our help and trust. It seems to fit them so well at times. So I advise you to identify your villains and move on.

Take Care Of Yourself

There's a tragic story in the news today of a Good Samaritan who stopped to help a stranded motorist and lost his life while doing so. What compounds this tragedy even more is he'd only been wed a few hours earlier. I mention throughout this book how important it is to be careful as we do good works and not just that we're habitually wary people by nature. Even when a wary Samaritan is busily about the business of doing well, the world around us with all its faults, failures, mistakes, ill-will, and accidents goes on. Enjoy your Good Samaritanism; but do take care. I don't believe there's some kind of magical shield which surrounds us as we go about God's business. God gave us sound minds and reasoning abilities so we'd exercise them at all times... especially when we're stepping onto the roadside to assist.

Some Days Many... Some Days Few

Don't despair in the hard times where trouble seems all about. You should look diligently on such days for examples of "Man's humanity to man." Some days there are many examples, some days there are few. This should not stop you from looking for them. I've never had more than a day or two in a row pass without spotting some positive effort where the fresh deeds of Good Samaritans once again came into view.

There Are No Small Good Deeds

Remember... to anyone who's desperately in need of a Good Deed, there are no small Good Deeds!

Charities And Survival Of The Fittest

There are days which wear down any wary Samaritan's patience. Routinely I'll go out of my way to help some offbeat charity make ends meet. Sometimes I donate money, sometimes I donate time, and sometimes I donate materials. I've shared with you elsewhere in this writing about being stunned by the lack of flexibility of charities which will simply tell me, "You'll have to take that with you, we don't accept them." I've heard similar stories from other would-be Good Samaritans.

The approach I'm taking is not to get upset; after all every charitable group has a right to establish their own guidelines regarding donations. Similarly, every donor has a right to establish her own guidelines about what charities she'll support. I understand some of the donation rejections I've received, but why does a charity two blocks down welcome the same donation with open arms? Charities, you really need to think about your mission, your vision, your tactics and integrating the three.

Would be donors, you need to examine a charity's mission, vision, tactics, and their integration of the three before you jump in. It may be there are other charities out there which are actually more aligned with your personal philosophy and more accepting of your means of support than some you're being rejected by now. These are fiscally hard times we're experiencing; weaker nonprofits will die off in a survival of the fittest mode. Redouble your efforts to support those who survive the die-off, but only so long as their mission, vision, and goals align with your own.

Thy Weaker Brother

As a young man I was taught, "You who are strong should bear the burdens of the weak." As the years have passed this wary Samaritan has often thought about what this means and who the weak and the strong appellations pertain to. One group which is easily overlooked for consideration as occasionally being in need of some bearing up are those people who've been born with deficits of one sort or another which make their life a constant struggle.

I'm thinking of those born with developmental disabilities ranging from those living within the Autism spectrum, to those moderately to severely intellectually disabled, and also those whose minds developed fully but their bodies never did. If you're looking for people who could use the help of a Good Samaritan from time to time, when you're feeling strong, please consider these to be among the most deserving of a hand from a strong brother or sister.

Finding Energy In The Good Works Of Others

If you as a wary Samaritan are constantly searching for positive things upon which to focus, looking around you for people performing good deeds can be a regular source of inspiration. I find at times our daily lives are so inundated with negative information one has to be careful not to become depressed or otherwise brought down by this flood of negativity. This is why it's more important than ever we seek out "Whatsoever things are good, whatsoever things are lovely, whatsoever things are of good report." Hang in there! There remains a beautiful side to life and Good Samaritans everywhere need to seek it out to remain energized and full of good works.

Move Along With Your Cheap Drivel

I had a teacher more than forty years ago who harped incessantly about "Man's inhumanity to man." In reflection I don't recall anything tangible he did which changed any of man's inhumanity to man, which calls into question the validity of his complaint. He had ample time to complain openly about this issue and did so routinely. Today this aging wary Samaritan understands talk is sometimes an inexpensive substitute for personal actions. It gives the talker an appearance of occupying the high moral ground while requiring he or she actually put forth no real effort.

If you're out there every day reaching out to others in need and putting yourself on the line, I'll hear your criticism and your complaints willingly. Those who are in the trenches doing the heavy lifting required to make the world a better place deserve to be the ones speaking out on those issues. Ironically the heavy lifters are seldom the most vocal. Who has the greater moral authority here? The critic whose only effort is criticism or the Good Samaritan there on the roadside ministering to those in need? If you're solely a critic, never raising a helping hand, move along with your cheap drivel.

Animals Need Good Samaritans Too

This wary Samaritan has two dogs, Chihuahuas both. In each instance they were rescued. The most recent came from our county animal shelter and in the older case from a friend in Bakersfield whose ill health forced her to leave her home and move cross-country to live with her children. She still misses him and checks in to see how he's doing; he's been with me six years now.

I want to salute all those good-hearted people out there who work daily to try and make the lives of animal's better by creating and supporting animal rescue efforts of all sorts. Yes, I know there are a few mental cases that end up on the evening news and make everyone trying to help animals look crazy. Thank God they're the exception and not the rule.

For better or worse, many Americans are bonkers about their pets up until the moment they aren't crazy about them anymore and choose to cast them away. When this happens, if it weren't for these Good Samaritans who take to heart the plight of unwanted, neglected, and discarded pets, the abandoned or neglected pet situation in America would be far worse than it is today! Animals need Good Samaritans too.

Sharing And Receiving Knowledge

A wary Samaritan learns mentoring young people is both an honorable and valuable way of being a Good Samaritan. Passing along our skills and knowledge to those in generations behind us is a time-honored tradition around the world. It not only assures the continuation of our societies, it strengthens the bond between the once young and the soon to be old, with the young men and women on whom they'll one day depend, either directly or indirectly.

For you who are growing old, you must be quick to share what you know when you find a receptive young mind. The days will come when your memories won't be summoned as easily as they are now. For those youngsters growing into the age of responsibility, be quick to receive the wisdom of those who've passed along this road before you. The day will come when you'll wish to ask a question of an older would-be mentor, only to realize they've already passed along this road and won't travel your way again.

Opportunities To Serve

My son-in-law Jake shared with me recently he was a volunteer in a senior care facility; he's volunteering to read to patients. He told me how gratifying he found it and how the seniors seemed to genuinely love it. I was struck by the connection between these seniors loving to be read to, little children loving to be read to my Daddy repeating an old adage, "Once a man and twice a child." Both reading efforts seem to me worthy examples of Good Samaritanism.

My guess is there are both senior care facilities and public or private schools in your area where you could volunteer to be a reader to seniors or children. Being a Good Samaritan requires full use of your imagination as you strike about looking for ways to live out your beliefs. Don't be put off by the organization's need to be sure you're safe to bring aboard; a background check and a little volunteer training is a small price to pay for the opportunity to make a difference.

As I say throughout this book, not everybody in need is lying on a roadside from having been set upon by bandits. When I was a child I was ill a great deal due to asthma, tonsillitis, upper respiratory infections, and ear infections. I spent many days alone in bed. Alone because I was always a responsible child, we were terribly poor, and Momma couldn't miss work to be with me. I didn't always have books for company. I can confirm the aloneness and wearying of empty hours; they're torturous for both young and old.

I've worked around the elderly for the last 40 years. Loneliness is one of their greatest battles; parents and siblings die, spouses and friends die, and if they have children, they may live a thousand miles away. Even if family and friends are nearby, there's no guarantee they'll visit. Clinicians and caregivers in senior care facilities are overworked, underpaid, and they're chronically understaffed. Frequently the patients only outside contact to hope for from day to day is a weekly visit by some church group, civic group, or a person like Jake. Is this an opportunity for you to serve?

It's Demanding To Be A Good Samaritan

Wary Samaritans are often amused when some newly minted Good Samaritan confesses to how a good deed she's done was actually laborious, or expensive, or time consuming. I always counsel this is to be expected since the first Good Samaritan labored, expended his own money, and gave generously of his time. So suck it up buttercup and settle it in your mind; it's demanding to be a Good Samaritan.

Stealthy Samaritans Take Care

As I've shared with you in other passages I've a habit of picking up nails, screws, and other sharp objects out of the street. No it's not because I'm an inveterate hoarder and want to take them home, though my daughters might argue the point. It stems from my belief if those kinds of objects were removed from streets and parking lots all over the world there'd be fewer flat tires, fewer automobile accidents brought on by low or flat tires, and people would save money avoiding needless tire repairs or replacements.

I'd guess there are a lot of other seemingly disconnected Good Deeds one could perform which would have similar outcomes. Look around your world and see if you can find a way to be a Good Samaritan in a stealthy fashion. As always, remember to do whatever you do, safely. When I pick up sharp objects from the street, I have to make sure I'm not going to be hit by vehicles. So whatever Good Deeds you find may also have inherent dangers; take care!

Never Counting The Cost

As a wary Samaritan I've had a lot of time in my life to consider the various aspects of the personality of the original Good Samaritan. It sticks with me the original never asked anything of the man he lifted from the roadside, despite it having cost him at the least time, money, personal risk, and emotional involvement.

Additionally, let's not forget the fact he likely had business of his own which needed to be taken care of that day, yet he set it aside and asked nothing of the one whose life he'd saved. Consider his selfless example the next time you feel put out when you've expended yourself and your resources to help one of life's victims.

He Led With His Heart

Three of the nicest aspects of being a Good Samaritan are, 1) you don't have to wait on anybody else to act, 2) you don't have to get the consent of a committee, and 3) you don't have to take a politically correct approach. I remind you of this, especially those among you who are looking at the world around you and thinking about what a mess it is. So far as I can determine the Good Samaritan didn't wait for others to act, didn't ask anybody's permission, and didn't question whether or not what he was about to do was politically correct. I warn repeatedly throughout my writing and speaking on this topic about the dangers associated with being a Good Samaritan and the need to reason a matter through. Yet even I can't deny the original Good Samaritan appears to have led mostly with his heart.

How Will Others Be Affected

Don't get so carried away trying to help one person you disadvantage many others. I saw this happen yesterday at a traffic light at one of our city's busiest intersections. Cars exiting a shopping center and attempting to enter the traffic near the intersection became stranded and couldn't get into the flow of traffic. My approach has always been to allow a single car in ahead of me before I proceed. A wary Samaritan has a part to play, but he's not the entire cast of characters. Imagine my delight upon seeing someone up ahead let a car enter.

Now imagine my dismay as the same driver allowed three more to enter, slowly I might add, only to force at least seven cars lined up behind this driver to miss the light. At an intersection like this one, this act can mean another three to five minutes of waiting. People who missed the light were inconvenienced without any say in the matter whatsoever. I find people don't seem to get upset over me allowing in a single car, but I could see the driver ahead of me pounding on his steering wheel and hear him honking his horn when he was stuck in traffic by this would be Good Samaritan.

We've been encouraged by the sages over the centuries to never allow our good to be evil spoken of. Wary Samaritans must be thoughtful and considerate of all people around us who'll be impacted by our deed and not just the single one we've become fixated on. This person waiting for so many drivers while others were unreasonably inconvenienced is an example of how to give any religion or philosophy a bad name. Please think before you act next time, lest your impulsive gesture of good will turns out to be anything but the positive you'd hoped for.

Wary Of Myself

I received some angry feedback when I originally wrote in my blog about people undertaking to do a good thing when they haven't thought the act through completely, and it doesn't turn out as they'd hoped. Just because you or I have good intentions as we launch otherwise well-intentioned efforts doesn't mean in retrospect we or others won't see mistakes or damage we made in the actions we took. We're not immune to criticism or even legal actions for failed or misguided efforts.

As I've stated before, I'm not only a wary Samaritan because I'm afraid of the stupidity, avarice, or malice of other people. I'm a wary Samaritan because of concerns about my own impetuousness, pride, foolishness, and ability to make childish mistakes. We ought to demand honesty of others, but the first party we must demand honesty from is ourselves. Always do your best to consider the aspects of your actions which are foreseeable. We can't be psychics, but we can circumspect in our actions.

Rough Patches, Potholes, And Bridges Washed Out

Only a long term Good Samaritan has a true grasp of how foolish people can be. This comes about after making years of effort in the area of good deeds, only to see a large portion of your effort wasted due to the foolishness of the person or persons they were intended for. This can be a crushing time and it ends all such future efforts by some Good Samaritans. When this moment finally hits you, you have two real options regarding how you'll go forward.

The first option is to throw up your hands, become disenchanted, and abandon all such future effort; you're a burn out. The second option is to become a wary Samaritan. With option number two you don't throw up your hands, you don't become disenchanted, and you don't abandon all such future efforts. Wary Samaritans resign themselves to the imperfection of all humanity, including themselves, and choose to love and serve humanity anyway. Here you're not burned out; in the parlance of the metallurgists you're tempered.

So the next time you're tempted to take option number one, but instead you choose option number two, congratulations you've moved from the place where you're a sometimes Good Samaritan, onto the path way of the fledgling wary Samaritan. Wary Samaritans adopt a much more informed approach to their Good Samaritanism. The road is not any smoother there, but your new found ability to accept rough patches, potholes, and bridge wash outs will greatly empower your journey from this day forward.

Bitter Good Samaritans

There are moments when it really hits a wary Samaritan that in order for her to allow someone else to go ahead of her in line, there is the corresponding fact she'll be moved back one spot in line; most of the time this means almost nothing. Once in a while it might mean not only are you disadvantaged temporarily, it could mean you're disadvantaged for the rest of your life. It's one thing to be put out for a moment, but to be put out for a lifetime is another matter.

In extreme cases Good Samaritans have been seriously injured or killed living out their values. It happens frequently when Good Samaritans choose to get involved in evolving emergency situations. Good Samaritans have drowned while attempting to save others from drowning, been killed by drunk drivers while assisting at an existing car wreck, and have been burned to death rushing into a burning building to help victims already trapped there. This Good Samaritan stuff is serious business.

Less dramatically, picture allowing someone ahead of you in the line and it turns out they want to buy lotto tickets and going for a random quick pick as you would, they hit a huge jackpot.

Not every case is this extreme, but you get the picture. My advice to you is to think these matters through before you get to this point and not after. Values are the rules we live by regularly. Values have an intrinsic cost and the cost should always be counted. Otherwise, you might spend the rest of your days a bitter Samaritan.

Allow God To Be The Judge

A wary Samaritan discovers in time it's better to be so busy in doing good deeds one doesn't have a lot of time to spend analyzing one's own good deeds. I'm not always the best judge of my effectiveness; I suspect there may be others who struggle with the same problem. After years spent fruitlessly trying to figure this all out, I concluded my best approach would be to do the best I could with regard to reaching out to others and then allow God to judge it all in his time. I don't necessarily have a clearer picture today about my effectiveness than I did before I took this 'let God judge it' approach, but I'm not nearly as anxious, self-defeating, or unhappy as I was when I regularly anguished over whether or not I was performing the quintessential good deed.

Suddenly A Victim

I'm struck this morning with the realization the Good Samaritan was himself exposed to the same elements as the victim he chose to help. For whatever reason, they were passing along the same path as they journeyed to some destination. I have to wonder if this crossed his mind as he spied the injured man lying there on the roadside. By the same token, perhaps you and I should allow this thought to enter our own minds when we encounter folks in need of a Good Samaritan. We never know at what moment life will turn in such a fashion we're suddenly and unexpectedly transformed from Good Samaritan to helpless victim.

Supporting Roles

My youngest daughter Rachel and her husband Dave are both involved in the entertainment industry; my son-in-law's role is in film distribution. Over the years they've lived and worked in Hollywood I'd wager I've come to know a great deal more about the industry than most people. This knowledge has made me more aware than ever how many people in the region actually work in the entertainment industry; it's not just the actors and actresses there. Once I was very pleasantly surprised to see the name of an old high school classmate.

Through the children I've met some actors and actresses. However, I've met far more accountants, lawyers, clerks, producers, directors, electricians, prop builders, secretaries, and innumerable assistants of every sort. It's gotten where I'll actually stay after the movie ends and the credits roll just to see if I recognize any of the dozens of names listed there. Occasionally I'm pleasantly surprised and have even seen the name of my old high school friend and Best Man a few times.

In the fifty years before the daughter moved to Hollywood it never occurred to me how many people it takes to make a movie, television show, play, or concert successful. As I've considered this information now for more than a decade, it's struck me this is similar to how being a Good Samaritan works. Their numbers are legion, they're mostly anonymous, and without them many of the wonderful things in life we take for granted would never happen. Unfortunately, there are no credits to roll at the end of each day to help us see how important their work is.

I was formerly involved in the church and Christian ministry for twenty years; fourteen of those years I was the senior pastor. I can tell you for a fact the church in all of its permutations is only successful because of unsung and unknown Good Samaritans. Not only do they faithfully serve their houses of worship, they live out their beliefs in their families, jobs, neighborhoods, and extended communities. They're the volunteers at the homeless shelter, parent teacher associations, alumni groups, sororities, fraternities, and free clinics.

In their even less formalized roles they're out there jumping dead batteries, pushing stalled cars, changing flat tires, mowing a widow's lawn, and rendering first aid at accident sites. For the most part their efforts go completely unnoticed, except by those who are directly affected. As I've said in my other writings and elsewhere in this book, they really are the social lubricant which helps keep all the gears of our complex society meshing. It's a testament to them the vast majority do not seek recognition and are often embarrassed by it when it's thrust upon them.

It's unfortunate there are no credits which roll at the end of each day on a giant screen in the sky, so the rest of us could better appreciate the work of the Good Samaritans in the world. I do believe at the end of life there's a judgment. As a Christian I believe how we've acted and reacted with regard to the savior is the key issue. But I also believe running closely behind this matter is the issue of how did we live out our faith. The Apostle James is credited with saying something along the lines of "Show me your faith without works and I'll show you my faith by my works." I think he was onto an important truth right there.

CHAPTER 12

Engage And Remain Engaged

I mention them frequently in writing and speaking, but one of my favorite charities is an organization called *ECHO* (Educational Concerns for Hunger Organization). They're headquartered in Fort Myers, Florida and their work involves creating and teaching methods to improve agriculture in the developing world. The kinds of appeals I've received from them tend to be with pictures of an improved variety of bean, a vitamin laden tree leaf which will thrive in the tropics, or a method for using waste grasses and crop residue to feed a digester in order to produce methane for a cooking stove. Yes, it's all pretty mundane stuff. But the thing I love about it as a wary Samaritan is once a gift is given to their efforts, it continues to give and grow exponentially.

As someone who's spent a number of years in agriculture and actually owns a company which manufactures and has sold thousands of tons of soil amendments and fertilizers here in the United States, I can say with definity our first world agricultural methods will not work for a family farmer with a half an acre on which to raise enough food or fiber to provide for his or her family. These farms lack the money, education, or technological support required for first world methods. This is why efforts like *ECHO* are priceless to these families, their communities, and their countries. I'm notoriously cheap and like for anything I'm working with to be cost effective. *ECHO* has amazed me time and again with how much bang they get for the buck in the long term

>www.echonet.org
>ECHO
>17391 Durrance Road
>Fort Myers, Florida

Trolls With You Always

We often say things, make gestures, or perform Good Deeds with only the best of intentions. However, a wary Samaritan soon notes an ongoing modern day trend where no matter how well intentioned an action was, there'll be critics in the form of Internet Trolls. One of my daughters wrote a short article for a national publication last year which was meant to be encouraging to young mothers such as her. She's a wife, a mother of three, and owns a successful business.

Most of the comments she received in the following days seemed to get what she was saying, but it pained me to see there were a few that seemed to be particularly vitriolic. Their vitriol was far out of proportion to the issue I might add. She's a grown woman and she, her sisters, and I have pretty thick skins. What I worry about are those more timid souls out there who try to say things, make gestures, or perform Good Deeds who are then skewered by the Trolls (in person or on the Internet) who then decide to give up.

The Trolls won't go away! They've been with us since the garden of Eden and they'll be with us until the final trumpet sounds. Just as surely as you could always find Jesus with a rapt audience, the audience always contained Trolls. So try to be strong, stay sweet in your soul, and recall the savior himself seems to have had plenty of loud and angry critics throughout his public life. If you think about it, if everything about your life were saccharin sweet, where would the savor be? Some ancient and life balancing advice says "Beware when all men speak well of you."

Staying Ahead Of The Trolls

It occurred to me after writing about Trolls yesterday, and their work in the present and throughout history, Trolls of one sort or another are the antithesis of the Good Samaritan. They only seem to exist for the sake of creating ill will, discontent, and injury. This realization helped me to see how Trolls have been on the rise for the past 30 years. I suggest you and I will need to increase our efforts as wary Samaritans if we're to stay ahead of the Trolls.

Best Supporting Good Samaritan

As a boy I was never much of a basketball player, but my lifelong best friend James "Weasel' Williams always was. Over the years it got to where my major contribution while the two of us played other duos to a game of 21 was that I'd feed him the ball and he'd score. My contribution rarely ran more than 4 points out of the 21. Once in a while I had a hot streak and scored as much as 6, but it was exceedingly rare.

Over the years I came to see assisting him really was the best role for me to play in these basketball games and so I became fairly adept at the assist. There are times in your efforts to be a Good Samaritan the very best you'll have to offer is an assist. We can't always be the scorer. Besides, what would a superstar be without teammates who provided the much needed assist? Don't ignore the opportunity to assist or look down on people in supporting roles.

I'm Not Pollyanna

I've been at this Good Samaritan business for more than fifty years now and so have many of you who are reading this book. I don't think my memory is quite as good as it was back in the 1960s, so when I encounter an old scam with a new twist it often takes me a couple of minutes to make the connection and cautiously begin to ease back from the precipice of here we go again.

At times I have to fight with myself to continue to care and try to make a difference in the face of so many well-practiced deceivers; my guess is some of you do this as well. However, I learned and accepted long ago I'd be taken in now and again and this is just the price you pay for caring and trying to make a difference in the world. In fifty years this hasn't changed; I suspect it won't if I should live fifty more.

Consequently, there was a time where I became deeply discouraged with the whole Good Samaritan business. I eventually found my way again and my overall enthusiasm for this life style hasn't waned since. I find the good you and I accomplish, both separately and together, remains more than enough to keep the world upright for another day. I'm not Pollyanna and you shouldn't be either.

Not Always An Easy Thing

I was asked recently if the Good Samaritan would've been a passive sort of a man. I was amused as I thought on this because each wary Samaritan knows from personal experience how much intestinal fortitude is required to take on the mantle of the Good Samaritan... and not toss it aside after a brief fitting. The passive don't last very long in this arena.

If it's in your heart to be a Good Samaritan, then accept now unless you have deep resolve, in short order circumstances will steal away any desire you have to perform good works. I've seen this happen loss of desire so often I now hold it as an inviolate truth. I believe every Good Samaritan who survives to become a wary Samaritan learns to count the cost of his or her good deeds and moves ahead despite the price!

Facebook® Panhandlers

As a wary Samaritan you've been approached by panhandlers a hundred times or more in your life. They adopt various guises or personas to ply their trade and you've likely seen each of them more than once. You know the hungry, the homeless, the disabled veteran, the stranded driver, and a dozen other variations on the old "Brother can you spare some change" routine. The fact is most of us have seen all of these and seen them so often we no longer even have to think much about it before we either pass on by or politely say No. Here's a good time to remind you there's no need to be rude, unless they're members of the aggressive panhandler school of begging, then you may have to be less than kindly in your response.

The newest breed of Panhandler took me a good deal of time to catch onto. When I first heard about Facebook® I resisted even looking at it because I'm naturally wary of the newest technologies; I like for someone else to be the Guinea pig in these social experiments. But once Facebook® had been out there for a while I embraced it and some other similar social media platforms. Over the first three years, due to years in ministry, health care, and academia I amassed several hundred friends. I wasn't very selective in who I accepted as friends so long as we had some real world connection. They were former parishioners, students, employees, classmates, relatives, and in general all the same kind of people who've friended you on your Facebook® page.

Over time I pared this list down to about two hundred. This came about due to peoples' wanting to argue about religion, politics, child-rearing, mental illness, dog grooming, and pretty much anything else after they got loaded or drunk for the evening. As the list of friends got smaller I did see something begin to stand out more than it had when I had three times as many posts to sort through. I started to notice the Facebook® Panhandler. I call them this because I began to see some people were expert at a very subtle form of manipulation where they were constantly reaching out to their Facebook® friends to come to their aid. It took the form of veiled pleas for money, transportation, food, and cash. They also posted pictures of their dilapidated car, threadbare clothing, run down house, and sad sack selfies of themselves or their children.

Now allow me to say when I see this kind of request out of someone once or even twice I'm not wary; we've all had times of need where these kinds of request can be perfectly legitimate. Where I did and do become wary is when it becomes a steady drum beat of unmet need. Eventually I dropped my personal Facebook® page completely for two years. When I did restart it I limited it to less than forty people I know and have known for decades. They're my family, friends, co-workers, and in most cases fellow wary Samaritans. I'm not opposed to Facebook® and hope you're able to use it positively. Simultaneously I do hope you're perceptive enough to know some of your Facebook® friends will use you. They'll do so just as long as you don't catch on to the fact they're playing you. When you finally unfriend them, they'll find new marks.

Compelled To Good Samaritanism

Some days a wary Samaritan can't find a break. Today as I was passing through the drive-through of a local eating establishment, I noticed one of their large plate glass windows appeared to have been vandalized and the rubber insert which secures the pane in the frame had been mostly pulled out and was dangling. I've built a building or two and my guess is this pane would cost a couple of thousand dollars. The other concern is that it become dislodged and injure someone. This one was in the playground area where young children could be seen happily dashing about.

When I arrived at the drive-through window to pick up my order I asked the young lady there if I could speak to her manager; I assured her she was not the source of my inquiry when her face turned pale. When the shift manager came to the window and I tried to explain the problem, she wanted to know if I wanted them to hire me to fix the window. I assured her I had no interest in the task. This only seemed to add to her puzzlement. Apparently she'd learned wariness of another sort in her job there.

I finally just said, "Ma'am, I'm trying to save whoever owns this franchise some money and perhaps avoid a serious injury to a child. I'm not sure this will matter to you as a shift manager, or that it will matter to the general manager you've assured me you'll pass this information along to. However, I guarantee whoever is the ultimate owner of this franchise will want to know how they can save this much money from disappearing off their bottom line." She looked bewildered as I took my order, thanked her for her time, and drove on.

One of the hardest things to learn, and I still don't accept this truth well, is that often a Good Samaritan will try to help people, and for any number of reasons the attempt at providing help is thwarted. Sometimes you'll later see your efforts failed to make a difference because they were never acted upon. If you're acting as God's servant in these matters, it's not up to you to decide who you reach out to. It's your lot in life to feel this compulsion to reach out and want to make a positive difference. Beyond this your conscience is clear and you just have to move on.

Critics And Rejection

In response to a question about having your good deeds criticized and rejected, may I remind you almost all of Jesus' good deeds were criticized and rejected by someone. If a master is the subject of intense criticism and rejection, can his servants hope to do any better? A wary Samaritan eventually adopts a creed which holds it's foolish to think you can go forth doing good and not have critics or rejection.

Critics are an indication we're stirring things up, we're attacking the status quo, and we're going against the flow. Unless you see something in the story of the Good Samaritan which I never have, this work invites critics and most often the criticism comes from those who passed by the guy in the ditch and didn't lift a hand in the first place. Often those who were best positioned to help, but didn't, will be your most ardent critics.

Rejection can spring from a hundred different sources and requires discernment to locate its true source. It can be born from the recipient's anger, pride, embarrassment, misunderstanding, etcetera, etcetera, etcetera, ad infinitum, ad nauseum. Surprisingly, outright rejection is sometimes more painful to endure for wary Samaritans than is criticism. I suspect this comes about due to our intense desire to help and the sense we've been thwarted in the effort.

You need to build a thicker skin in order to survive as a wary Samaritan. Critics will be a factor in every aspect of your life. If you had siblings, you know this starts early and stays late. Rejection is something you must have met in childhood; who hasn't been rejected from the sports team, the in group, or the object of one's affections? These are normal if painful facts, which don't go away just because we wish it so.

Take A Closer Look
Being a Good Samaritan is either a lifestyle one embraces or eschews. I don't recall my first good deed, but I'm sure it came along long before it became part of my earliest cub scout training. I'd have been less than eight years old. Some people I talk with about Good Samaritanism embrace the concept while others are aghast at the naïveté of someone who feels like it's a good thing to go out of your way to help total strangers. I understand their mindset; it's a mindset wary Samaritans have consciously rejected.

A wary Samaritan continues to see a world in need of more Good Samaritans, not fewer of them. When I engage in conversations along these lines, the other side's arguments inevitably boil down to a cost/benefits analysis approach tied to dollars and cents. I like to remind folks not all of the costs and benefits in life can be solely equated in dollars and cents. It seems we've abandoned the concept of good works being emotionally or spiritually rewarding.

I'm not sure how to properly compare the self-centered mindset of this age with regard to putting ourselves out for others, even to the limited degree wary Samaritans put themselves out for total strangers. I recognize this is confusing to many and perhaps even repulsive in a hedonistic age. But the truth before us remains people have observed and adopted the Good Samaritan mindset in increasing numbers for more than two millennia. If you're not yet one of them, perhaps it's time for a closer look.

Accept And Celebrate You

I've been reflecting today on what kind of man or woman takes on the mantle of the Good Samaritan. I'm convinced it's an entirely different mindset from the usual religious crowd. As I reflected on this it occurred to me the Good Samaritan appears to have traveled alone. Now in those times a journey of any distance over public roads was much safer if taken in the company of a group of like-minded individuals (e.g., merchants, priests, scribes, soldiers, etc.).

Now it could be this man had no friends. It could be this man had such a unique trade or craft he had no equals similarly situated. Or, it just could be he was one of those gregarious souls who marched to the beat of his own drummer at the time and pace so dictated. Give some thought to this and what it is about you which makes you willing to be the one who leaves the well-travelled roadway and goes down into the ditch alone. It's okay to march to a different drum, so accept and celebrate you!

Good Samaritans In Every City

I was genuinely heartened today to hear of several people in New York City helping a pregnant woman deliver her baby on a sidewalk, once it became obvious the time to get to a hospital had come and gone. People not only stopped and got involved, they offered up scarves and coats to cushion the mother and to wrap and shelter the newborn. Despite the evil we hear about constantly in the 24/7/365 news cycle, there are still Good Samaritans in every city.

Something Positive In The Air

For a second day in a row I've seen news of another tremendous outpouring of Good Samaritanism in New York City. The photo circulating on the Internet showed a police officer on the ground with an obvious gunshot wound to the leg and several Good Samaritans gathered round him shielding him, comforting him, and rendering first aid. It does my heart tremendous good to see people reveal their true selves in time of crisis. God bless these folks and all the others this week who've taken the harder course and gone onto the roadside to care for another human being, who couldn't otherwise care for their self.

Unsung Heroes

All in all, it's been a great week for Good Samaritans in the news. I know there are thousands, perhaps even millions of good deeds done every day by Good Samaritans who are never noticed, much less get their name or picture in the news. I can't guarantee if you spend your life being a Good Samaritan anyone will ever notice you or the efforts you've made, but I can guarantee you at the end of your own life you'll know you did what you could for your fellow man.

Children Of The Same Creator

I witnessed a man guiding a travel trailer as it backed out of vary narrow lane at the gasoline station at Sam's Club®. At first I thought nothing of it until the task was finished and the driver of the trailer stepped out to shake the other man's hand. I had assumed the two were in the same vehicle and the passenger was merely guiding his driver. However, the driver of the trailer was clearly an African-American. By the dress of the stranger guiding him, I would venture he's a member of our large local Sikh community; I also noticed the symbol from the Golden Temple decal in his window as he drove away, which further confirmed my surmise.

I raise these touchy issues of race and religion here for a specific purpose and not just to be obtuse. I don't believe Good Samaritans are limited to the Christian community or any particular race. In the course of these many years I've learned Good Samaritans come in all races, religions, colors, and ages. I've experienced this first-hand more than once. This universality of the desire to do good deeds should really come as no surprise, since we're all the children of one God. I'd say if one is a bigot of any sort, and since God has a sense of humor, he might well send a Good Samaritan to the rescue which challenges the rescuee's racial or religious prejudices.

Doing Nothing At All

Sometimes the kindest deed you can do for people is to simply leave them alone. Judging when to intervene and how to intervene in another's life is a delicate undertaking. Through mostly trial and error across the years I've gotten better at this, but like most wary Samaritans I don't have it down to an art form, much less a science. Consequently, I think in terms of there being a time to act, a time to wait for action, and also a time when I should do nothing at all.

Social Media Con Artists

Allow me a few more minutes of your time to discuss a phenomenon so pervasive in this era I almost forgot to mention it in this book. Because of my age I've lived about half my life without computers and other similar devices being readily available to the public. For younger readers seeing this work you'll never have known a time when there weren't personal computers, laptops, tablets, and some type of cell phone or smart phone. The advent of these devices and the social media it's spawned changed the lives of wary Samaritans in both positive and negative ways. The positive was the ease with which we could share information, call attention to local or national crises, and with which we could electronically raise funds for worthy causes. The negative has been in the fact all of the old confidence gamers, scammers, and phony beggars were rapid adopters of the technologies.

There are tens of thousands of legitimate charities in the United States and around the world doing good work. They dedicate themselves to meeting the needs of the hungry, homeless, sick, dispossessed, and forgotten peoples everywhere. In some instances they've been doing this for a hundred years or more; they're not the Johnnie-come-latelies at this dance. Just as surely as legitimate organizations and good-hearted people utilize social media, con men, scammers, and professional panhandlers have adopted social media and adapted their evil to make the most of it. You no doubt are already aware of some of them because some of them are so clumsy and obvious in their efforts, only the dullest among us would be fooled. If these clumsy practitioners were the core of the problem, we wouldn't have to make much of an effort to avoid falling victim to their chicanery.

As the level of sophistication of all social media has elevated, so has the level of cleverness and deceit employed by these wolves in sheep's clothing. Not only has the level of sophistication among them evolved dramatically, the decrease in the cost to utilize social media has placed professional levels of technology in the hands of people who heretofore would've been limited to begging at the freeway off ramp or from some ramshackle storefront church. The number and type of scams I see being run on the Internet these days is almost impossible to count. Tens of thousands of charities now have web sites, YouTube® channels, Twitter® feeds, and as many other technologies as their IT department can dream up. Where media ministry presences were once limited to organizations large enough to raise the capital to buy television or radio time, today they can be livestreaming on the cheap in a day or less.

As is always the case, mixed in amongst the thousands of doers of good deeds there'll be those who use the cover of charity or ministry to plunder the unwary. The other area where I'm seeing this, which absolutely appalls me, is in the proliferation of pseudo-scientists and pseudo-physicians out there. I recently read an expose on a fellow who claims to be a self-taught physicist of sorts. He claims to have figured out a means to obtain a free and limitless supply of energy. The man's followers regard him as a genius. In fact, some of his followers have made sizeable donations to his research, research which has yet to produce tangible results, which can be independently verified. This isolated incident is sad to me, but what compounds it is there are dozens of other pseudo-scientists and pseudo-physicians out there making equally outrageous claims and taking people's life savings.

As a researcher who's worked on a good deal of chemical patent research and prototype development, I'm always cautious of inventions which seem too good to be true. As a former pastor, I'm always cautious of ministries and mystics making fantastic claims which seem to defy all schools of theology and common sense. As a former health care administrator, I'm always cautious of medical devices and medications which have never been peer-reviewed while making claims of miraculous cures. However, even if you have none of these back grounds, as a wary Samaritan I suspect your wary Samaritan sense tingles much of the time when you encounter one of these oddities on social media. I have no plans to abandon social media; I hope you don't either because as I've said before in this book, it has tremendous potential for good. Be as careful in considering social media solicitations as you'd be if approached on the street with the same offerings.

Please Check The Math

I had another encounter with one of those roadside math problems today. It's a math problem where you see facts which don't add up. In this case it was another disabled, hungry, and homeless Veteran begging by the roadside. He was on the island at one of our city's busiest freeway off ramps. What didn't add up was this aging Vet was missing a leg and would have accordingly qualified for some form of either social security or disability social security.

The emaciated and bedraggled and near-toothless appearance of his younger female assistant didn't add up either, unless we're talking addictions.

Now he may well be a Vet, he definitely has a disability which would qualify him for all sorts of assistance programs here in California. But my guess is all those dollar bills he and the young woman assisting him were gathering at the freeway island were likely headed to buy drugs and/or alcohol. Alcohol and Meth are twin epidemics in California. Here in central California we each see so much of this it's not hard to spot. If you've worked with addicts, as I and many of you reading this have, you can spot them a block away. Please check the math before you help buy a daily supply of alcohol or Meth.

Lighten Up On Yourself

This wary Samaritan, like most wary Samaritans, second-guesses himself a great deal regarding both sins of commission and sins of omission, especially when it comes to matters of my own Good Samaritanism. I can remember people I did not reach out to from years past and often wonder what happened to them. I can also recall some I did reach out to, which turned out badly and wish I had no such memory.

I suggest to you after years of living with these two extremes of not doing enough and doing too much, each of us has to do the best we can and then live in the hope in the long run the good we did far outweighs the bad we unintentionally did. There's a tendency amongst this crowd to be self-flagellating. Lighten up on yourself; you likely already have enough outside critics without you joining in.

CHAPTER 13

Otto Davis

Scattered in this book you've encountered a few personal tributes to people who reached out to me in true Good Samaritan fashion and made a huge difference in my life. The last one I'll mention of those people was an old neighbor of mine named Otto Davis. When my family moved into the house, which continues to be my home, back in 1964, the Davis family was already living in the house immediately East of ours. The family consisted of Otto, Viva, and their grandson Clovis. The Davises were from the Midwest my family, as my family was. But whereas my father was a farmworker, Otto had been an oilfield worker and had even owned his own drilling rig.

I knew the grandson Clovis much better than I did Otto, though Clovis was four years my senior. The first summer I lived there Clovis and I built a white picket fence between our yard and theirs. We've remained friends for more than 50 years. Clovis had come to live with his grandparents after the death of his father. The grandparents doted on him and being an excellent student, an eagle scout, and a star athlete had made that all the easier. Otto and I on the other hand had what could only be described as an odd relationship. Here was someone I saw at the time as just another gruff old man, doing his best to have conversations with a hyperactive pre-teen.

I was shocked when I was twelve years old and he began to invite me to go to the oilfields with him on Saturdays. I wasn't even sure he really liked me and just figured he put up with me because I hung around with Clovis. But confusing as this was, he began to take me out to the oil lease where he had a part time job as a 'Pumper'. If you don't know the oilfields, the best I can tell you is a Pumper is the person who makes sure the oil gets out of the ground, in the tanks, gets cleaned up, and finally sold to a refinery. In those days it was considered a plum job and generally reserved for men who'd spent a long and knowledgeable career in the oil fields.

So, on random Saturdays when I didn't have a football game, basketball game, or track meet, I'd pile into his old Chevy pickup and make the journey 20 miles south to the Tejon Oilfield. Every time he'd have me come with him to gauge the oil levels in the tanks, check the oil wells, pack stuffing boxes which might be leaking oil, bleed waste water from tanks, and grease any squeaky pumping units which pulled those dragons from the ground. This usually took up an hour at most. At this point he'd always tell me to take the sack lunch I'd brought, explore the hills, and watch out for rattlesnakes. This routine went on for some years until high school, athletics, and chasing girls won out for my attention.

I never really gave this whole scenario much thought until I was an old man myself and reflecting on my life and the people who'd helped me become the man I am today. As a very young-married 19-year-old, I happened to interview for a job at the lowest possible rung of the ladder with an oil company. The job paid a whopping $3.50 an hour; exactly twice what I made at my fruit packing house job as a mechanic's helper. The Superintendent of the company was pleased with my mechanical and welding skills, limited though they were, but he said the job entailed more than just mechanical work and welding; I was crestfallen. He said what he needed was someone with some other skills.

As I was preparing to leave the interview he said, "Have you ever been around the oilfields Farrell?" I brightened and said, "Yea. My neighbor was a pumper and used to take me out on weekends to pump his lease." Suddenly I had the Superintendent's attention. He asked, "What kinds of things did you two do?" I was puzzled but responded, "We gauged tanks, we bled tanks, we packed stuffing boxes, we greased pumping units, we tested crude oil samples, and we filled in his daily logs." "Did he let you watch him or did you help him?" I thought about it for a moment and replied, "The first times he only let me watch because I was scared. Afterwards he showed me how and then let me do some of the work. After a few months I could do it alone but he always watched me." I wasn't expecting anything to come of this until the Superintendent said, "I'll tell ya what... I'm gonna take a chance on you. Can you start next Monday?"

It hit me for the first time the other day, almost fifty years after the fact, Otto Davis had been teaching me; I never even realized it and he never said a word about it. There were no chalkboards or formal lectures. Within a few months of my hire I was given a raise to $7 an hour. Within six years I would have my first $100,000 earnings year in the oilfields. I went on to be a field foreman for one of California's largest independent oil companies and worked in oil and gas on four continents in the years since. It opened the doors which have led me to where I sit today. There could be, there would be, no Dr. Farrell Neeley if it wasn't for people like Otto Davis who saw me on the roadside destined for a life as a farmworker, and unobtrusively extended a helping hand.

Sometimes Only Words

Like most of you there are times in the checkout line at the local market I'll engage another shopper in conversation. Tonight I chatted with a one-year old while her mother loaded her purchases on the belt. The baby giggled and made faces at me as I interacted with her, but out of the corner of my eye I could tell by the number and quality of items the young mother was buying, she wasn't a one-percenter.

Eventually, she finished her check out and paid with an EBT. She kept her head down and refused to look at me or any of the other shoppers as she concluded her transaction. The load out belt was spilt in two halves and I was finishing up my single bag as she loaded up several of hers. It startled her when I spoke as I was leaving, "You have a beautiful little girl and she has a great personality. I attribute that to the fact that she has a very good mother."

The young woman's head lowered slightly, her eyes immediately showed tears, and she never spoke as she walked away. Sometimes, the words of a Good Samaritan can be as powerful as any deed. We can't always take physical action. But almost every day we can speak words of encouragement to people around us. People need to be supported in the crushingly mundane issues of life, which at times can suck the spirit right out of any of us. Mark your words and use them well!

For All The Good You Do
My youngest daughter's blog today suggested giving out little cards or other awards which recognize people's good deeds. As a wary Samaritan I think it's a wonderful idea; Good Samaritan's have never gotten enough recognition for all the good they do.

Good Deeds And Good Samaritans
In a news feed earlier this morning I saw details of how a man had gone into a Starbucks in east Texas and plunked down four hundred dollars to "pay it forward" for other people. When asked why, he said it was because he loved to see people happy. The article went on to say many others joined in the spirit of the day and added some of their own money to the four-hundred-dollar starter this gentleman put up.

Good deeds and Good Samaritans come in all sorts of shapes and sizes, races, ethnicities, religions, philosophies, and under all sorts of circumstances. I suspect there are times you've had an impulse to make a generous gesture like this one, but felt self-conscious. Have you ever considered how self-conscious the Good Samaritan felt getting involved after the important professional and religious folks had passed the problem by?

There's More Than One Kind Of Good Samaritan
I love those stories of the retired school teacher, or janitor, garbage man, or gardener who'd lived frugally all of their lives, invested their savings wisely, and upon dying it was revealed they'd left millions to the local school, library, church, or Boys and Girls Club. Good Samaritans come in many different shapes, sizes, and flavors.

Some are routinely about the business of being a Good Samaritan throughout their lives, while others may have the desire in their heart to be a Good Samaritan for a lifetime, yet only be able to live it out after their life comes to an end. I've learned over the years to be slow to judge others and to appreciate all kinds of Good Samaritans with equal joy.

Action Not Words

One of the quickest ways to get injured or killed is to intervene in a domestic dispute of some sort. I learned this when I was a young man just trying to understand the life of a minister by accompanying my pastor on house calls. During the 14 years I was a senior pastor, I saw it in all its permutations. I've seen women nearly killed by their lover, husband, spouse, partner, or whatever else you want to call them. The worst part of it, I saw it in my own home as a child and even then I couldn't simply turn away and not try to stop it.

Today as I was coming through the old neighborhood driving to my home, I saw a young man with a young woman; she was holding a baby in her arms and the young man appeared to be striking her in the head with his fists. As I neared them he broke off the attack and they both immediately acted as though things were normal. After a moment or two, I drove on but decided to circle the block. When I came back, once again he was working over her arms and shoulders with an occasional shot to the head. The site of a man beating on a woman sends me instantly over the edge. I witnessed my Father periodically hitting my mother; it ended only when I was 16, fully grown, and he saw the deadly rage toward him in my own eyes.

I drove directly toward the young couple and he moved away. He paused for a moment acting as if he was going to stand his ground, but the sight of a one-ton truck now headed directly at him set him running. The girl made her way in the opposite direction and into the courtyard, apparently hurrying toward one of the little apartments clustered there. She wasn't bleeding and the baby appeared to be okay, so I waited a few minutes to be sure the boxer didn't come back. I drove the three blocks onto my home. I didn't call the police because in a neighborhood such as mine, heavy with people here illegally from central and south America, there's little or no cooperation with the police on the part of the victims.

In that moment the words attributed to Edmund Burke, which we've all likely heard many times came to this wary Samaritan once again, "The only thing necessary for the triumph of evil is that good men should do nothing." There are moments where this comes sharply into focus, as it did for me today. Talking does little good when people's lives are immediately on the line; I think the legal term is exigency. There come times in life when immediate action is the only course which will make any tangible difference. I know not everyone will go so far as I have and I do; to those who have and will again, I say be wary because in these instances you truly put your life on the line.

Blessed Is He Who Is Not Offended In Me

For those who tend to involve themselves in the lives of others, there's nothing more personal than to take an interest in whether or not people have proper nutrition; this is a polite way to say whether or not people are eating properly. I tend to err on the side of being proactive in this area and sometimes I give food to people who actually don't need it; it happens perhaps one or two percent of the time.

My point to you here is there are many people, including working families, who are struggling these days to feed themselves. I choose to be embarrassed for trying too hard, rather than not trying hard enough and then finding out later a child went hungry because I was afraid I'd offend their parents. For those one or two percent who express no need, I simply encourage them to pass some along to those in need.

No Less Important
You'll find children are in need of a Good Samaritan at least as often as adults, if not more so. The crises little ones live through are not always matters of life and death, but they're no less important to the child. Each wary Samaritan learns a compliment, a word of encouragement, the gift of five dollars, or even the willingness to just stop for a moment and hear a child out can make a real difference across a lifetime of such encounters.

Allowing Others To Serve
Long ago I learned it's important to allow others around you to be the strong one sometimes, even though the issue of the moment might be easier for you to handle than for someone else. I'm not suggesting you stoop to pretending to be a victim, but you don't always have to be the strongest Good Samaritan on site. If you do, other younger would-be Good Samaritans never get a chance to break out from beneath your very large and experienced shadow.

You Could Lose Your Good Samaritans

Many Good Samaritans are routinely taken for granted, or they've been about their effort at performing Good Deeds for so long and so quietly they've become invisible. A wary Samaritan notices this most often in organizations, but especially in houses of worship and service clubs. We see how people have given of themselves to such a degree their efforts have become expected and invisible.

The way this is usually exposed is some member passes away or gets transferred to work in another city and suddenly the coffee isn't made, the floors aren't swept, the grass isn't mowed, or the newsletter never got published. People are forced to stop and consider who used to do those things and in making the calculation they're often shocked at how they took those efforts entirely for granted.

Look around your place of worship, your club, your alumni group, or even the workplace and you soon realize the most important grease in the gears kind of people are often taken for granted. It becomes embarrassing when they simply wear out and die or quit due to good deed fatigue. Organizations of all sorts need to identify and support their Good Samaritans. If they don't, they may lose them.

Blessed Are The Peacemakers

Jesus said, "Blessed are the Peacemakers…" and I'm prone to agree at every level of life there are not enough of them. We need peacemakers in the home, school, church, workplace, local government, state government, and national government. The truth is there never seem to be enough of them to go around.

So if you're one of those Good Samaritans who's gifted as a Peacemaker, this wary Samaritan salutes you!

The True Good Samaritans

Lest you should begin to worry about running out of places to exercise your Good Samaritan instincts, you can always recall Jesus' words, "The poor you have with you always." Now I'm not talking about folks who want, I'm talking about poor folks with genuine need. Yes, I know there are many who feign poverty or may even choose poverty for the sake of a life of free benefits. No matter how cynical you may be from a lifetime of encountering grifters and con men, never get it in your head there aren't genuinely poor people who need your and my help.

In every generation there are those around us who are genuinely poor and need our help. I often say "I'm a wary Samaritan, not a cynical Samaritan." I do so because once you cross the line into terminal cynicism there may be no coming back. I've seen this occur with ministers, social workers, psychologists, educators, and law enforcement personnel; it's never pretty. So later today or early tomorrow, I challenge you to begin to attempt to spot the truly poor around you; perhaps even in your own neighborhood. The rest of it will come easy to the true Good Samaritan.

Lending Them A Helping Hand

There are people out there who make extra money, or make their only money, by recycling aluminum cans. You see them rummaging through trash cans around town and in the alleys behind businesses. I know a few of these folks and regularly offer them whatever empty cans I have when I encounter them. I shared elsewhere here how my wife does the same.

Some time ago I stopped one of these gentlemen at the dumpster behind my wife's business; the gentleman my wife often assists works the front of the building. As we exchanged the cans, he said, "You know, I used to work in this shopping center." I think he saw the surprise in my face and went on, "No! Really, I worked at the little restaurant across from your wife's shop until the economy went sour and they laid me off because business was so slow."

"I do this," he said while motioning toward the dumpster, "to stay alive. I'd love to have a regular job again, but no one is hiring right now for guys like me with just a little schooling." He seemed desperate to explain and ended by saying, "I still got my pride and selling cans beats begging to me." I admired the fact his initial effort wasn't looking for a handout; I could see his personal pride was still intact.

As he got on his old bike to ride away, I had a new insight into how deeply the economy has tanked and as a result how many people out there can use a true helping hand. Be on the lookout for others in similar circumstances in your area, and where you can safely do so, lend them a helping hand. We should always consider the recipient's dignity first before we accidentally strip people of their own sense of personhood.

Watch For The Quiet Ones

I got to wondering yesterday how many people I've passed by in my lifetime who were experiencing true need and I never recognized it. I've encountered many people who can't stop telling you about their troubles; over and over and over again. The folks who never speak up are the opposite side of this coin. For whatever reason they've come to the place in life where they're stoic about their situation and will die before they speak up for themselves; my mother was like this. Caring professionals everywhere wish these stoic people would step forward and acknowledge their need before it kills them. But for whatever reason they rarely do so.

We most often find out about their need after it's too late to make a difference in their lives. A case I'm personally familiar with involved a highly educated and beloved man I knew who died for lack of basic medical care which you and I would take for granted. It was a minor surgery performed thousands of times a year on an out-patient basis. He'd become an alcoholic, lost a stellar teaching career, and didn't want people to know he had a serious medical problem and no medical insurance; his death still haunts me. For this reason, I challenge every reader here to pay special attention to those you come in contact with who never indicate any personal need.

The quiet ones, the cheerful ones, and the seemingly happy ones may be the people you meet who have the greatest needs but can't or won't speak up for themselves. You and I must go the extra mile required to look deeper than the surface and to take more than just a passing interest in those who appear least needy. When the man mentioned above died and was memorialized, more than two hundred of us came to his memorial. Everyone who attended was devastated they hadn't known he needed medical help and wouldn't ask anyone for help. This included me who assumed he knew I was a giving person and would've gladly helped if I'd only known. Tragically, we lost a really good man.

Avoid Her At All Costs

I make mention elsewhere in this book of intervening in a domestic violence episode and cautioned about the inherent danger in efforts of the sort. Let me step to the other side of the intervention scales and say you must also be careful your intervention isn't just a matter of trying to project your personal preferences on other people. The faith crowd sometimes struggles with this.

If you intervene in a matter where the law is clearly being broken (e.g., assault, battery, robbery, rape, burglary, murder, etc.), the law will support you and I'm on your side. But if you inject yourself in personal matters involving choices (e.g., clothing, music, language, etc.) and no law is being broken, you're likely to end up on everybody's "Avoid her at all costs" list.

Needs In Front Of Your Face

From time to time, I'm asked by some older person to assist them in resolving some kind of business issue where they need to gain computer access and they don't even own one, much less know how to use one. I try to get these folks to sit next to me while I make the contact on my laptop so they can see how easy it actually is. If I can do so I'll even get them to play with the keyboard and the touch pad a bit so they can see it's not going to injure them and they won't break it.

I take the time to do this because I hope the experience will spark some new level of interest. Isolation is one of the major problems with aging and becoming old. We have fewer and fewer living friends and relatives and even they can be hundreds or thousands of miles away. Computers, smart phones, iPads®, Skype®, and the Internet have created a means where people can easily be in contact with friends and family all over the country and all around the world.

I challenge you to consider taking on this kind of good geed, or something similar, as a way to make older people's lives fuller, more meaningful, and less isolated. Yes, I'm sure there are other ways to do this and I encourage you to find them and adapt them to your circumstance. I've said many times before being a Good Samaritan requires one be aware of his or her surroundings. If you can't or won't pay attention to the world and the needs around you, there's no point in fantasizing about meeting needs half a world away.

Life's Hard Questions

Superficial relationships are a hallmark of our times. We all become expert at being able to casually pass and re-pass with folks we know without every knowing more about them than the most obvious superficial facts. I've come to believe this is the reason so many people live with serious unmet needs in the midst of societies with relative plenty. They're ashamed to say, and we're embarrassed to ask. I learned as a young pastor if you would be a Good Shepherd, sometimes you have to ask the hard and uncomfortable questions in order to uncover the unmet need. I extrapolate this concept here and suggest if you would be a Good Samaritan, sometimes you have to ask the hard and uncomfortable questions in order to uncover the unmet need.

Recognizing Other's Good Works

Like most Good Samaritans I receive nearly as much satisfaction out of seeing someone else do a good deed as if I'd done it myself. It's been said we should delight ourselves in good works.

I'm pretty sure this doesn't mean just our own good works. If this is indeed the case, we should both encourage others to do good works and we should honor their good works with our own recognition of those good works. You and I are not the only two people on the planet about this business of good works. It takes nothing away from you or me to recognize and honor others for the good they do.

Look Before You Leap

One of the worst things you can do as a Good Samaritan is stay at it so long and so hard you burn out. As a wary Samaritan I encounter good-hearted and well-intentioned men and women all the time. Some of them have become weary and cynical over the bad experiences they've had while trying to do good. Every Good Samaritan who's been at the task for any appreciable length of time has been burned. The getting burned part is what made me wary, but it didn't make me quit. Pace yourself, learn from your past mistakes, and when the opportunity arises again jump in. But next time look around and figure the situation out a bit before you leap.

Horrible Things Sometimes Happen

People who know me personally and not by reputation alone know I've taken my share of bumps, bruises, and beat downs over the years as a Good Samaritan. It's for this reason I get the occasional call from someone who is beaten down, who's been referred to me by a friend. The discouraged Good Samaritan who calls is usually not only discouraged, but likely traumatized by some unexpected turn of events as they were trying to live out their faith. Some have been slandered, some have been robbed, some have been assaulted, some have been battered, some have been raped, and some are calling because they or a loved one, often a long time Good Samaritan, has been hospitalized or killed.

It's a dangerous world out there. I'd be lying to you if I pretended it wasn't. To this date I have never been raped, hospitalized, or killed for my efforts. It doesn't mean those couldn't happen, it just means they haven't happened yet. I've experienced all of the others, and each of them more than once. There are other violations I didn't even put on the initial list; you'll find your own. Many of my longtime friends who've chosen to live the same kind of wary Samaritan existence I do, have experienced similar events; my experiences are absolutely not unique. I always advise people to enter and live this life with their eyes wide open. Bad things happen to Good Samaritans... horrible things sometimes happen to Good Samaritans.

Wisdom And Resolve Are Both Required

I've warned in my other writing and elsewhere in this book about allowing a Good Deed to become a source of problems for others. This is a tough area to judge as my next sentences will demonstrate. It's a happier variation on a scene I described elsewhere in this book of a courteous driver allowing too many people to enter traffic ahead of her, thus forcing hardship upon others. As a wary Samaritan you'll need to be able to take the pulse of the situation you find yourself in so you don't become a burden instead of a blessing. Again, we're admonished to be wise as serpents and harmless as doves.

I watched today as a driver allowed two other cars to enter traffic ahead of him. They had been cutoff while attempting to exit a shopping center next to a traffic light. Allowing two cars to enter traffic takes more effort, thought, and resolve than simply allowing one. People may begin to honk and you may start to get nervous about what you've done; I know, I've been there. I was pleased to see the thanking waves from the two entering drivers, greeted by a huge smile and an acknowledging you're welcome wave, from the Good Samaritan. In this case fellow waiting drivers took it with grace.

No Big Issues Here

Each wary Samaritan knows people who want to be Good Samaritans, but the would-be Good Samaritan specifically cautions God and anybody else who'll listen, they don't want to deal with any big issues. This amuses me and other wary Samaritans because we can almost hear God laughing at their request. If you've bought into this journey, once the ride starts, you get the full 'E' ticket treatment. There are no stops, except at the end of the ride on the Good Samaritan roller coaster. You younger readers may have to ask your elders what the 'E' ticket statement meant.

It's Not About You

A wary Samaritan learns whenever she does good deeds it shouldn't be motivated by her personal need or how it makes her feel. If we reach out to others because we live for some sort of endorphin-induced high, then our good is not about the good it does for others, or the good it does for the Kingdom of Heaven, it's really about the way it makes us feel about ourselves.

This doesn't mean it's wrong to be happy at the outcome of good deeds. We should experience joy in our good deeds because we put the same level of love and concern out each time we act as Good Samaritans. Shouldn't true joy come from living out our values? Shouldn't true joy reflect the spiritual recognition of having personally embraced God's law at its deepest levels?

Examine Your Own Heart

I address this issue often in person and here again in writing, perhaps more often than some would appreciate. I contend if you're unable to be a Good Samaritan within your own family, neighborhood, or nation, what makes you think God is calling you to some other locale or distant foreign land to carry out the role of a Good Samaritan there? This is generally seen as my criticism of people reaching out to those in need in other countries, it's a myopic view of the critics at best.

I'm as wary of other Good Samaritans as I am of those who need a Good Samaritan. I'm from the old school, this is the one where we're charged to routinely examine our own hearts to see what it is which truly energizes our existence. It's not always noble when we examine our hearts, is it? Sometimes what we find there is both ugly and petty. Sometimes our actions are more about how they make us feel, where they take us to, or the adulation generated as others view our apparently selfless efforts.

Call it prayer, meditation, or daydreaming, but by whatever name you call it engage in some routine, honest, searching of your own heart. Africa, Asia, Europe, North America, and South America all need missionaries; to this end I've supported missionaries monetarily for 45 years. I do sincerely worry the Good Samaritan who can't or won't reach out to his or her own family, community, or nation is not the ideal candidate for evangelizing the world with Christ's message of love, hope, forgiveness, and salvation.

It's Their Decision... Good Or Bad
This wary Samaritan advises you can only offer your own example and if people will not heed it or adopt it, the outcome is on their shoulders and not yours. This may annoy you, anger you, grieve you, or exasperate you when others chose another way of conducting their life than the one you feel is best. It may even be a terrible and destructive way they choose to go, but people are free moral agents and have to make their own decisions, whether they're good or bad. As a Good Samaritan you're not God and you're not any other Good Samaritans final judge. You're in fact just one of God's very minor and highly fallible agents. Think on these two facts whenever your opinion of yourself becomes inflated.

The High Cost Of Friendship
Perhaps the most expensive thing a Good Samaritan can do, next to laying down their life for someone else is to befriend a person in need. True friendship isn't just a passing thing bound by feelings of a moment. Some may think they can dart in and out of people's lives, but people in need seem to have a way of being in need again and again, and they'll need a friend going forward and not just for a moment. I advise other wary Samaritans to hold friendship in reserve as one of your most precious assets. Friends are powerful individuals, whether they realize it or not, and while it's easy to slip into a friendship, it's incredibly difficult to disentangle oneself in trying to escape a friendship gone bad.

Diversity Of Good Deeds
A wary Samaritan learns it's difficult to precisely define a good deed. The reason being, what seems a good deed to you might be something unwanted or even distasteful to someone else. It's

because of this important truth I once again caution all Good Samaritans about drawing conclusions or making judgments about the good deeds of another. We each live our own lives, come from our own places, and carry our own experiences. This makes each Good Samaritan as unique as a fingerprint. Accept this as a truth and you'll be happier for it: "Diversity of Good Deeds is a good thing."

Gain A Friend

Let me suggest there are times when the very best good deed you can do is to catch a mistake someone has made and quietly correct it before it becomes a crisis. A wary Samaritan learns through the years everyone makes mistakes throughout their lives. Most of them are minor mistakes, some are moderate mistakes, and once in a while we'll find ourselves having committed a huge mistake with equally huge consequences. Try as you might, perfect as you think you are, this will happen to you.

In the work place, church, or your club, there are people who have your back and there are others from whom you have to watch your back. Determine early in your life as a Good Samaritan to be from the "I've got your back" school, there's always a surfeit of the other group anyway. Life is hard enough without feeling like others are hoping you make a mistake so they can crush you. When you can be a Good Samaritan and catch a mistake before it erupts into crisis, you've gained a friend.

Be Careful What You Say About The Dead

Even when you know evil things about someone, it does no good to speak of such evil at any time; we've all got plenty to answer for when the final judgement rolls around. Remember your role as a Good Samaritan and remind yourself this is never truer than when people have died. Here's a short verse to help you with this. "In remembering the dead be kind in what you say, for just as sure as you're alive right now, you'll be dead someday."

I encountered an elderly man (any man older than me) at the Barber shop I regularly frequent. It was the first time I'd ever met him though it soon turned out we were raised in the same town. During the course of the encounter and the ensuing conversation it happened to come to light I'd known his oldest brother, a friend of my father's, when I was a young teen. We chatted for perhaps five minutes as he finished his haircut and I sat down in the now empty chair to start mine.

When he'd shuffled on out the door and it clicked shut behind him one of the other patrons said, "I recognize you and I know you're an old preacher... now if you knew his brother, you know he was rough as a Cob... a gambler... a drunkard... a skirt-chaser, and a notorious brawler." I nodded my head in agreement and said, "You're absolutely right. But you don't have to focus on the very worst things you know about a man when you talk of him with people who love him." It silenced my questioner.

You might want to think about these words as your life moves forward. Not every chapter of the book of any of our lives is flawless. One of my favorite rhymes, which I had to learn as a school boy, is one I share often. Now would be as good a time as any to share it again with you. "There is so much good in the worst of us, and so much bad in the best of us, it ill behooves the most of us, to talk about the rest of us." May you live a life where most of your deeds are good and most of your failures are tiny.

CHAPTER 14

The Most Wonderful And Dangerous Time Of The Year

I used a 14 month cycle in writing this book originally, hence the 14 chapters. Christmas that year actually came along in month 12, but during editing I moved the writing here to chapter 14 because I wanted it to stand apart from the rest of the book as something you could turn back to easily each year when Christmas time came along in order you could easily find and review it. I specifically use the term Christmas rather than Holidays because Christ is at the very center of Good Samaritanism.

Like many of you who will read this book, I didn't have the greatest childhood in the world. We were a poor farmworkers family to begin with and my father's chronic alcoholism made certain we'd never rise out of that poverty. I suspect that many of those childhood Christmas seasons and the sadness and chaos they often brought to our home have played an inverse and disproportionate roll in the development of my own Good Samaritanism.

But rather than being drowned by this, I fought through the years to work beyond my annual "Christmas blues" to find a happier way to experience the season. It was in fact my deliberate decision that I would enjoy Christmas each year going forward and that I would work to help other people enjoy it as well that, that seemed to have dissolved my annual melancholy. I found that by reaching out to others at Christmas, the holiday was a joyous one for me. This is one of the key truths of Good Samaritanism.

I learned a couple of important lessons about this time in my life. First I learned Christmas really could be the most wonderful time of the year. People's desire to be kinder and gentler seemed to affect the atmosphere. But the second thing I learned was that evil people understand that kinder gentler people have let their wariness guards down and can be more easily taken advantage of at Christmas time than almost any other time in their lives. Unfortunately it makes it a dangerous time of the year as well.

My hope is that you'll be able to enjoy the Christmas season in its fullness. My hope is that you'll reach out to others at this time in an expansive way. My hope is that you'll be energized in your mind, body, and soul by this beautiful respite period at year's end. But my greatest hope is that the things you experience as you give of yourself to others at Christmas time will make you want to expand the effort and carry it on throughout the year. The world can be a brighter place and it's up to you and I to make it so.

Finally, the story of the Good Samaritan is the story of Christmas in a different form. Jesus, the son of God, was that Good Samaritan. He witnessed the world having been set upon by thieves, beaten, robbed, and left for dead and could no longer ignore what was happening. He'd asked the religious crowd to reach out for years; they walked on by. Seeing no one else who was willing for the task, he became flesh and dwelled among us. In time he offered up all he had to redeem us. He is the ultimate example to every Good Samaritan, especially the wary ones.

Before The Holiday Madness Begins

As I write this passage it's just before Thanksgiving and later this week the Christmas Holiday Season will swing into high gear. Before this happens I want to suggest a novel approach to your giving this holiday Season, though it's something which could easily be done throughout the year. I want to challenge you to set aside whatever you can afford to give to a needy stranger. For some of you it will be twenty dollars, for others one hundred dollars, and for a few among you it may be a thousand dollars or even more.

A few years back I felt God prompting me to give gifts of money to total strangers who were in obvious need. It had to be God because I'm not naturally so inclined. However, my first reaction wasn't born of disagreement, it was concern and embarrassment because I wasn't even sure how to do this without risking my life and embarrassing someone already struggling with enough of a burden in life. After more than one failed effort, I came up with a pattern which works for me; you can improvise on it as you see fit.

Carry the money you set aside in your pocket, wallet, or purse for when the moment of need appears. Make sure it's secure but not so secure it takes forever to access it. You're going to see them and God will help you recognize the genuine need in their eyes. Most years I encounter them at the supermarket; Mom's with children in tow. They may be looking wistfully at all the holiday food treats while pushing a near empty-basket of generic staples such as milk, cereal, and juice items; items you and I both know to be payable through WIC.

You could just as easily see them on the street, at your house of worship, the gas station, a school program, the post office, or in a shopping mall. You can use any approach you want to give them the money. I've found handing it to them with a simple Merry Christmas greeting, a very minimal explanation, and moving along quickly helps them and me avoid any feelings of awkward embarrassment. I admit such fear of embarrassment has stopped me at times in the past; I ignore it now.

On one occasion I've said, "I think you dropped this." I then handed Mom a hundred-dollar bill. The woman had four little kids and looked stunned as I was turning to quickly walk away. Whatever approach works for you, keeps you safe, and allows the recipient to leave the interaction with their integrity intact is a good approach in my assessment. Be wary, never be heartless. Now go celebrate and enjoy this holiday season more heartily than you've ever enjoyed it before.

Welcoming Kinder Gentler Days

You can't help but notice each year at Christmas time there seems to be a little less hostility out there and a little more of a willingness on the part of people to show some kindness and consideration for their fellows. Whether it comes about due to the nearing of the holiday season or simply because the days are shorter and people are at home resting more, I welcome it whole heartedly. After all, when the last two or three days before Christmas arrives our good natures will be fully put to the test as anxiety grips many shoppers and wary Samaritans warily anticipate visits from their family.

A Time For Joy And Caution
A day earlier than usual, holiday shopping has begun. The malls and department stores are filled with happy shoppers. Unfortunately, at this time of the year they're also filled with pickpockets, purse snatchers, and con men. As a wary Samaritan I've learned to love this time of year, despite all the ugliness from those with evil designs. My advice to you is enjoy yourself and your family, be cautious when you're out and about, and never stop looking for an opportunity to be a Good Samaritan.

Holiday Bell Ringers
A truly wary Samaritan should know some of those Holiday bell ringers are paid an hourly wage and some are not. I learned this years ago when my late son, Ryan, was a bell ringer one Holiday season. I was puzzled he'd taken on this bell ringing effort and one evening as he was leaving to tend his kettle I asked him why he was doing it. He told me what it paid per hour and then he told me he was donating all he earned back to the Salvation Army. Don't be so quick to judge those bell ringers. Some of them need the money just to make ends meet... and others of them have already decided in their hearts they'll give the money back to the mission!

Seasonal Good Samaritanism
I believe the Christmas Season brings out the Good Samaritan in a lot of people who don't normally show the tendency. My best advice to a seasonal Good Samaritan would be to give in to your inner Good Samaritan and reach out to those who are in greater need than you are. They'll be blessed, and you'll be blessed. Who knows, perhaps it will become a regular habit.

Receiving Goodwill

During the holiday season where we're all being extra attentive to those in need, be sure to allow room in your life for other Good Samaritans to be of service to you. This wary Samaritan believes if we don't allow other people to act on their positive impulses toward us by allowing and accepting their offers of help or tangible items, eventually their fount of goodwill may cease to flow. Always be as willing to receive as you are to give. This isn't about personal greed, it's about being willing to accept being the helped instead of the helping.

No Room In The Inn

At this time of the year, traffic all over the city is snarled and parking lots are stacked up like the 405 Freeway at quitting time. It was in this place in time I saw her. She had the misfortune to go into one of those small side parking lots off the gigantic main parking lot and was now unable to find a break in the traffic to exit back out into the main shopping center traffic flow. There were a dozen cars ahead of me when I saw her; I kept thinking someone would allow her in... I was wrong.

All these shoppers rushing home with their treasures didn't seem to have peace on earth or good will toward their fellow woman in this case, on their minds. When I finally got close enough to make out her features, she had children in the car and I could see the frustration she was fighting. When I stopped to let her in, it took 10 seconds for her to register what I was doing and the guy behind me honked... I ignored him. She waved as she pulled out into the lane and sped off into the gathering dusk.

Today It's Your Turn

Today the shoe was on the other foot as other drivers were the ones who allowed me into the flow of Christmas shopper traffic. My Momma always said, "What goes around, comes around." Be sure to sow some seeds of goodness and mercy as you make your way through life. And it never hurts to let other drivers get into traffic or merge into your lane as well.

Good Works Improve Your Outlook

Today was a better day to be a wary Samaritan than yesterday. When I've had a bad day, the next day I try especially hard to find a place to do good because it always puts me in a better frame of mind. In this instance I encountered a young couple in a big box store where the young man was struggling to land an extremely large box on one of those flat carts they use in all the warehouse stores these days. He was clearly upset and muttering audibly about the lack of service or help in the place. His female companion seemed to be a combination of amused and concerned.

    My first reaction was to walk away, but when I passed again in two minutes and he was still fighting the box, I asked him, "Can I help?" He looked me over for a minute and seeing I was at least twice his age, he replied, "Are you sure?" I assured him I'd be okay and bent down and picked up my end of the box. It was about five feet long and printing on the cover said it contained a portable basketball goal and goal post. Once we'd landed it on the flat car, a smile came to his face and he visibly relaxed. "Thanks" he said as he began to push his prize away.

    Being a Good Samaritan is as good for you, if not better, than it is for the recipient of your good works. I'm sure some physiologist could offer a scientific explanation involving oxytocin, serotonin, endorphins, or some such brain chemical required to elevate mood. I've never spent any time looking too deeply into the situation, preferring not to look a gift horse in the mouth. I'm satisfied the recipient went away in better condition than I found them and I went away feeling better inside.

Don't Let This Day Pass

You wary Samaritans out there occasionally make what appear to outsiders to be dumb efforts to be Good Samaritans, just as I do. I shared with some of my friends in recent days how I repeatedly brought empty shopping carts from the Sam's Club parking lot to the Sam's Club lobby on Christmas Eve. I did so because there were no carts available and it seemed like a good way to reinforce the Christmas spirit. As I write today, it's the very last day if the year on which I can be a Good Samaritan, I won't let it pass without making some effort, even if it appears dumb to others.

The Hardest People To Reach Out To

We only have a few more days to go until Christmas. I like to spend those days reaching out to those in need. Christmas is the worst time of the year to be struggling mentally, spiritually, or financially. It's bad to be struggling all year, it's worse at Christmas. In the course of all our revelry we should remind ourselves to be about Good Works every day of the year, as if it was Christmas. I hear voices from past ages reminding me to keep Christmas every day.

As a fellow wary Samaritan I know by this time of year many who are retired or have earned extended vacations are already on your way or have arrived at the places you will spend your

Christmas. Even for the best among us, this can be a time of high stress for the kindest and most generous people us as we gather with prickly family. Let this passage stand as a reminder to try to be just as loving and concerned this week with the people in your life who are often the hardest people in the world to reach out to... your family.

All Year Long
The most amazing thing I routinely observe on Christmas Eve is one shopper allowing another shopper to take the final item. Preferring our brother is an ancient concept. It's one which should be regularly observed and even more so during the Holy Days, whatever your belief system.

Christmas Is Definitely Over
A sure sign Christmas has passed is being on the 405 Freeway in Los Angeles on the afternoon of the December 26th as I was, to witness countless examples of rude drivers and road rage as the 405 became a giant parking lot. One I might add which stretched out for 15 miles. I don't know if this bad behavior should be attributed to the pent up anger of being sequestered with family, not getting the Christmas gift they wanted, or just overdosed and hung over from rich food and too much alcohol. I can say December 26th is always a good day to pray the New Year brings a return to a more civil society.

We Rarely Know
Just as the days left in any year tick down to zero, so do the days in our lives. A wary Samaritan decides at some point to try and spend life reaching out to people who need a helping hand.

Thanks to the calendar, we can know how many days are left in the current year. Thanks to clocks, we can know how many hours and minutes there are left in those days. However, we've no such device to keep track of the days, hours, and minutes left in our lives. Such awareness of what we don't know helps remind us of the need to be routinely about God's work; we rarely know when we're living our final year, day, hour, or minute.

New Year... New Opportunities

It's the day after New Year's Day and next week even those with the most extended periods of Christmas and New Year's vacations are likely to be back at their respective desks, computer screens, shovels, punch presses, or factory floors. This was evident today on any of the nation's freeways which are still moving and not already snarled by the latest winter storm.

Traffic was bumper to bumper as I was coming out of Los Angeles late today and it could only be the result of folks headed back to their regular lives in Bakersfield, Brookings, and Boise. Be gentle out there as you venture into your newest of new years and join all wary Samaritans in keeping an eye out for those who've fallen on the roadside in the coming year.

Author's Afterward

This book has been on my heart for more than twenty years. I hope by finally putting these words to paper I can now move on to the other topics churning in my mind. Our world is in desperate need of Good Samaritans. My long-term concern here is for the many people I've seen start out as Good Samaritans who became wounded, embittered, or killed off along the way. By writing this I hope to help some return to the path of Good Samaritanism and to help others avoid these tragic outcomes.

I've come to believe the only way for you and I to avoid some of these spiritual catastrophes is to operate as Good Samaritans, but to operate from positions of wariness; hence the term wary Samaritan. Wary Samaritans do not abandon their world. Wary Samaritans do not withdraw from their appointed field of battle. Wary Samaritans do not become bitter. Instead, wary Samaritans have learned that if they think things through before they jump in, they can do good and survive as loving caring people.

Once you've read through this book, I hope you'll pass it along to a friend. You could also buy them their own copy, keep this one, and come back to read these thoughts again, should you be looking for encouragement or to reorient yourself to the wary Samaritan lifestyle. In either event I hope this book has been enlightening and encouraging to you. As you have the opportunity, please consider buying my other books and coming to hear me speak when I'm in your part of the country.

    Farrell F. Neeley, PhD
    September 30, 2016

www.ingramcontent.com/pod-product-compliance
Lightning Source LLC
Chambersburg PA
CBHW051749040426
42446CB00007B/289